Wallace-Homestead
PRICE GUIDE TO
AMERICAN
Country
ANTIQUES

13TH EDITION

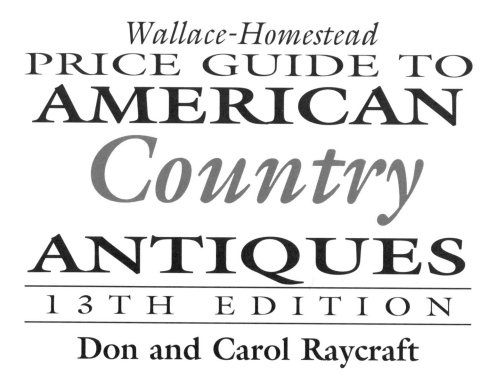

Wallace-Homestead
PRICE GUIDE TO
AMERICAN
Country
ANTIQUES
13TH EDITION

Don and Carol Raycraft

Wallace-Homestead Book Company
Radnor, Pennsylvania

745.1
RAY

To

the memory of our friend,

J. Maxwell Pickens.

He loved America and Americana.

Contents

Acknowledgments

Al Behr
Gary and Lorraine Boggio
Marian Charow
Gerald and Lorraine Coffman
Teri and Joe Dziadul
Jake and Jenny Elliott
Ken and Carlene Elliott
Michael Fallon
Richard and Ann Louise Ferguson
Garth's Auctions
Ray and Nancy Gerdes
Bernie Green
Rose Holtzclaw

Dr. Alex Hood
Brenda Humphrey
Barbara Boardman Johnson
Cathy McDonald
Opal Pickens
Tom Porter
Edie Preece
Ann Roop
Melissa Strang
Ellen Tatem
Bruce and Vicki Waasdorp
Jerry Jeff Walker

Photography

Michele Breedlove
Joe Dziadul
A. L. Ferguson
Brian Kaplan
Carol Raycraft

R. Craig Raycraft
Scott Sandler
Ellen Tatem
Bruce Waasdorp

Quilt Drawings

Melissa Strang

Introduction

Almost thirty years ago, when we stopped at a small antiques shop in the eastern Illinois community of Watseka, the owner of the business asked about our interest in early Americana. She had been a collector for twenty years, and in the mid-1960s, on the Illinois prairie, she was not finding many people who were interested in decorated stoneware, woodenware, and painted furniture.

She mentioned that she no longer collected much for herself, because soaring prices had taken the fun out of it for her. We were neophyte buyers then, and had no frame of reference for pricing Americana. When we entered the marketplace in 1965, the price or availability of a cupboard or pie safe back in 1950 meant absolutely nothing to us; our only concern was what it was going to cost us today. If a dry sink cost $200, we considered it only on the basis of whether we had the money to buy it, a place to put it, and a way to get it home.

Our experience did not include visits to dozens of shows, or hundreds of shops, to help us evaluate the price and quality of a piece. We had not "passed" on better examples for half the money two years previously in Pennsylvania. We had no "good old days" to influence our decision-making process. There were no price guides for Americana and "primitives," and few periodicals to consult for insight. Most collectors depended upon their own instincts and previous experiences, and at that point we had neither.

Thirty years later, we have been to hundreds of shops, shows, and markets, and we have more perspective about prices. We now find ourselves in the position of the woman who felt that prices had passed her by in 1965. We have watched prices double and then double again. In 1965 you could not make a mistake buying country furniture with an original painted surface, because the supply of merchandise so far exceeded the demand that there was no money to be made in creating reproductions. In some New England and Pennsylvania shops, if you asked a dealer if he had a dry sink with a painted finish, the response would be, "What color?"

In a recent antiques newspaper article about the current market a Vermont dealer commented, "When I started in business in 1962, I could take my vehicle any day and return with a full load, just from word-of-mouth referrals from home to home without ever knocking on doors."

Every collector who begins to accumulate country antiques starts from a different price perspective. The prices you are initially exposed to become your reference points for what follows. A beginning collector today who finds a refinished pine dry sink with a replaced back for $700 has never seen a blue sink for $150 or purchased one out of a barn for $85. But if you are someone who paid $12 (retail) for a bittersweet 6″ pantry box in 1970, it is almost impossible to force yourself to write a $225 check for a lesser example today.

The country antiques market is self-perpetuating because new collectors are constantly jumping on the bandwagon while veteran collectors with long memories are reluctantly getting off. It never stops. The merchandise gets harder to find, tastes change, and prices continue to increase, but those presently on their first trip around the block will look back at today as "the good old days" in thirty years and remember the items they should have bought and foolishly didn't.

We do.

1 *Buying and Selling Country Antiques*

The manner in which antiques are bought and sold in the United States has evolved considerably over time. In the early 1900s used furniture stores were replaced by antiques "shops." For almost seventy years collectors made their way from shop to shop and attended periodic shows sponsored by charity organizations in urban settings.

Antiques Malls

In the late 1970s early versions of the antiques mall began to appear in facilities that previously housed supermarkets, auto parts stores, or factories. The first antiques malls were designed to allow numerous antiques dealers the opportunity to rent a booth in the mall, stock it with their merchandise, and receive a check each month for the items that were sold. Some malls took an additional small percentage of the gross sales as a "seller's premium."

Antiques malls were almost an overnight success because they allowed customers to drive to a single well-lighted location and see 35 to 200 booths filled with merchandise. The business hours were posted on the door, and someone was always there. Most of the early malls had specific standards of quality for what they allowed to be sold. New items, collectibles, and crafts were not permitted.

Real estate agents who had clients with empty buildings to rent in suitable areas helped to start many more malls. The proliferation of new businesses generated pricing competition for space in some areas as well as increased competition for dealers; building owners in many instances had to lower standards to keep the malls open and filled with dealers. Crafts and collectibles dealers were recruited when necessary to keep the dealer roster filled because the turnover rate was often quite high.

Periodic problems with the economy from the 1980s to the present has cut down the amount of foot traffic and buying in many malls, generating anxiety and a continued mass exodus by dealers in some locations.

The antiques malls that have been consistently successful for owners and participating dealers over the years are those which maintain and enforce high standards of quality. Some require dealers to decorate their booths in room settings, or rotate the merchandise monthly, to give customers a reason to return and shop. As with any business operations, those that meet the needs of their customers will succeed and those that do not will fail.

Group Shops

In some sections of the nation group shops have been in operation for years, and in others they are almost unknown. The group shop concept involves a number of dealers who combine their resources to open an antiques business that operates within certain predetermined guidelines. All the dealers have responsibility for the operation of the business, and share in the expenses.

A group shop is similar to an antiques mall in the way the merchandise is sold. Each dealer receives the proceeds from the sale of his or her items. The advantages of the group shop are obvious: the dealers control the participants and the quality of merchandise that is offered for sale, and share the responsibility for the success or failure of the business. In an antiques mall the dealers are at the mercy of the mall operator and have only limited control over their own economic destinies.

It is apparent to us that the group shop concept will continue to flourish as antiques malls with marginal merchandise flounder. The key is to maintain the quality of merchandise that is offered for sale.

Capturing the Passing "Look"

In recent years there has been a growing tendency for many upscale clothing stores to fill their windows with American country antiques and collectibles. The various Ralph Lauren-Polo stores from Freeport, Maine to points West have featured a rural and sporting "look" in many of their display windows. The windows and instore decorations are generally well executed and cause passersby to stop and savor the contents. A natural question that arises is what effect the Polo stores (and countless others that have adopted the country look for displaying merchandise in their stores and print advertisements) have had on the antiques market.

Our considered opinion is that in the short run the effects have been minimal, and in the long run they will be negligible. There are major differences between antiques collectors and individuals attempting to capture a look. Collectors have a greater degree of commitment, some basic knowledge, and the periodic ability to spend considerable amounts of money for something they can't exist without possessing.

The casual shopper who wants to replicate the look in a window on Rodeo Drive or Fifth Avenue is less interested in authenticity, provenance, or information about the pieces to be bought because there will be other looks that will replace the current one.

Over the past several years there has been renewed interest in sporting collectibles. Windows of shops have displayed fishing tackle, leather football helmets, felt pennants, and baseball gloves, to create a mood and sell products. We have seen fifteen-year-old baseball gloves that went unsold at garage sales for $1.95 a year ago suddenly offered for $50 in antiques shops, malls and markets. It appears that some shoppers took the theme from the windows at the shopping mall home and incorporated some of the ideas into their personal decor; they liked the look and went in search of it. Antiques and collectibles dealers have cooperated by finding the merchandise for them and prices have risen accordingly.

The problem of an overabundance of sporting collectibles at severely discounted prices at garage sales is going to arise when clothing store window dressers move on to decorate with seed catalogues, checkered tablecloths, and cast-iron tractor seats.

Yesterday and Today

In case you haven't noticed, things have changed a lot since 1964. In 1964 Mickey Mantle was paid $100,000 a season to limp around centerfield for the New York Yankees; in 1994 he makes that much in a weekend signing autographs at baseball card shows. Thirty years ago the Beatles were leading the British invasion of American popular music; today the Beatles are among the most requested groups on oldies radio stations. In 1964 Vietnam was becoming a nightmare for many American families; today Vietnam is an emerging tourist attraction.

The antiques world has undergone almost as many alterations. The list that follows is a selected summary.

1964

1. *Country cupboards and dry sinks are still being carried out of barns, attics, and basements.*

1994

1. *The barns, attics, and basements have been replaced by parking lots of shopping malls and tanning salons.*

1964

2. The supply of merchandise exceeds the number of collectors looking for it.

3. The emphasis is on refinished pine tables, dry sinks, and cupboards.

4. Publications feature articles on a variety of topics ranging from carnival glass to copper cooking pots. Homes that are photographed often contain refinished colonial furniture.

5. Watering cans are still being sold at hardware stores rather than at antiques shops.

6. Antiques are sold in shops rather than malls.

7. Collectibles are sold in dime stores, given away to the Good Will, and found in the bottoms of cereal boxes.

8. Traveling to an antiques show is an event to savor.

9. The only place to buy crafts is at the retirement home a week before Christmas and Easter.

10. All the Shaker collectors in North America could hold their national convention in a telephone booth near Mt. Lebanon, New York.

1994

2. The supply of "honest" or "right" merchandise is considerably less than the demand for it.

3. Most collectors are searching in vain for country furniture with its original finish.

4. Numerous home furnishing magazines feature "country" and "colonial" antiques, collectibles, and crafts of varying quality.

5. Watering cans are being collected as a critical part of the country look.

6. Collectibles, crafts, and gum are sold in many "antiques" malls.

7. Collectibles have entire shows, malls, shops, and lives dedicated to their preservation.

8. If you randomly select any street corner in any town in America with more than 10,000 people, an antiques show will be held within a four block radius this weekend.

9. The only place crafts are not offered for sale is in an operating room of the Mayo Clinic in Rochester, Minnesota.

10. All the Shaker collectors in North America could hold their national convention in the honeymoon suite of the Rising Eye Motel in Niagara Falls, N.Y. Those attending still wouldn't speak to each other.

2 *Antiques 102: The Crash Course*

The purpose of this section is to provide you with the necessary background information to become a recognized national authority. As you know, doing this for you has become a lifelong quest for us. When the local antiques study group has a question or needs a guest speaker, we want them to call you. When regional meetings of jelly glass collector clubs are held at the YMCA, we want to see a snapshot of you standing at the podium.

To read this section you need a security clearance. When you bought this book you automatically received that clearance. If you have borrowed, stolen, or checked out this book, it is impossible to grant any level of clearance.

We would suggest that after reading this section you take a pen and cross out the key words, in order to make what remains unintelligible.

Some Fundamental Truths

A new collector can learn some fundamental truths, like the following, from us, without the consequences involved in learning each one from experience.

If buying an expensive piece of stoneware, furniture, folk art, or other item, make the purchase from a dealer who specializes in that particular item and who will stand behind it with a guarantee, in case it turns out to be less valuable than you originally thought.

If you are at a flea market or swap meet and the rarest item is a pair of white nylon stretch socks with orange stripes, immediately get back on the bus, drop in your three quarters, and go home.

If you looking for a place to dine after the antiques show, pick out a rotund exhibitor and ask him or her where the dealers ate last night.

If you have *any* concerns about a potential purchase, trust your first inclination and don't buy it. Don't hesitate to ask the dealer questions about a piece that interests you. The dealer wants to sell merchandise and has a responsibility to answer your questions (just remember, the dealer has no interest in learning that your Aunt Cleo went through life dressed as a Cub Scout).

Most dealers have an asking price for their items and a selling price; they will work with a serious buyer to establish a satisfactory selling price.

There are major differences between collecting antiques and accumulating collectibles. Several years ago *Sports Illustrated* magazine offered to its readers hundreds of pristine copies of its forty year old debut issue that had been found in a warehouse. Copies already in the hands of collectibles accumulators took a major jolt, because most were in a lesser condition and the market was saturated by the find.

Americana collectors do not have to worry that an abandoned warehouse filled with nineteenth-century dry sinks will suddenly be discovered in Cleveland.

Individuals who put away "Beverly Hills 90210" drinking glasses and Madonna notebook dividers as long-term investments may or may not be doing their great-great-grandchildren a favor. Only time will tell. The single certainty is that environmentalists and landfill operators are overjoyed with the collectibles mania. It keeps a great deal of garbage under the bed or in the attic rather than overflowing the dumpsters.

Buying at Auction

Most collectors eventually purchase something at auction. Whether the auction takes place in the backyard of a rural farmhouse in Iowa or in a carpeted New York City gallery, the following guidelines apply.

Because many auction firms have instituted a policy in recent years of adding a 10 percent buyer's premium to the selling or gavel price of each item sold, it is important that the potential buyer determine in advance of bidding whether a buyer's premium is in effect. For example, a cupboard with a gavel price of $1000 would cost the buyer $1100 after a buyer's premium was added.

On occasion an auction tends to turn into a contest between two individuals who have never met, over a $50 item of questionable age that they are competing to buy for $425 (plus a 10 percent buyer's premium). Before the bidding begins it helps to set the price beyond which you will not go. Do not exceed your predetermined limit in the excitement of wanting to "win."

Make it a point to go early to the preview and closely examine the items in which you have interest. If you question the age, finish, or degree of originality, let someone else buy it. If there is a potentially significant piece that you are unsure about, employ an expert to give you a second opinion. A $25 to $75 investment for such expertise, when contemplating a $4000 purchase, is a good one.

As noted earlier, you should have some idea which items you are interested in buying before you attend an auction. Many auction firms want your purchase removed from their premises as quickly as possible after the sale. If you have the slightest suspicion that you might buy a large piece of furniture, bring a van or truck, or make advance arrangements to get it home.

If you are a regular customer known to the auction house, you can probably write a check. If not, it will be necessary to have cash, a money order, a certified check, or a bank card. Find out in advance how the firm prefers payment. Before the auction you may want to establish a line of credit with your bank if there is a possibility of a major purchase. Regardless of the size of the sale or the extent of your purchase, you will need some form of identification.

Read carefully the "Conditions of Sale" on the poster, brochure, or flier advertising the auction. You need to know the rules under which you will be bidding, and how the auctioneer warranties the items that are being offered for sale.

Terms

absolute auction: An auction where the selling price is whatever the item brings when offered for sale. In an absolute auction there is *no* reserve or minimum bid.

buyer's premium: An additional percentage (typically 10 percent) paid by the buyer to the auction firm based on the gavel or selling price of an item. If a basket is purchased for $100 at auction, the buyer's final price is $110.

choice: If the auctioneer has a grouping of ten chairs or eight collectible bottles and says "Buyer's choice," the successful final bidder may select any one or more of the items, or buy them all for the price for one times how ever many he wants. This saves the auctioneer and the potential buyers from watching multiples of similar items being sold individually.

consignor: The individual who actually owns the merchandise being offered at auction.

reserve: A "floor" price established by the owner and auctioneer *prior* to the sale below which the item will not be sold.

Using Price Guides

The purpose of any price guide is to provide the reader with the approximate value of a given item. A price guide should be used much like an auction catalog that contains an estimation of an item's worth. The auctioneer includes an estimate to help potential bid-ders gain some perspective about values and a hint about what to expect to pay on auction day.

Our price guide assumes that the item pictured or described is at least in excellent, original condition and, unless otherwise noted, the value listed reflects that condition.

Each year we contact nationally known dealers, auction houses, and pri-vate collectors from diverse areas of the United States to establish values for American country antiques.

Values listed are the approximate prices the items are being offered for in a shop or mall, or the price the piece has brought at auction.

Ten "Must Read" Selections

We have searched through our li-brary several times to select a basic list of ten books that we feel should be part of every country and Americana collec-tor's life. You will note that we have purposely not listed any of the books that we have written, because there is no doubt in our minds that you already have those!

Some of the older titles may be out of print and will be found only in used book shops, at flea markets, or in the stacks of a public library.

1. Emmerling, Mary, *Collecting Am-erican Country*, Clarkson Potter, 1983.

2. Fales, Dean, *American Painted Furniture 1660–1880*, E.P. Dut-ton, 1972.

3. Gould, Mary Earle, *Antique Tin and Toleware—Its History and Ro-mance*, Charles E. Tuttle, 1957.

4. ——, *Early American Wooden Ware*, Charles E. Tuttle, 1962.

5. Kassay, John, *The Book of Shaker Furniture*, University of Massachu-setts Press, 1980.

6. Kirk, John, *The Impecunious Collec-tor's Guide to American Antiques*, Alfred Knopf, 1975.

7. Osgood, Cornelius, *The Jug and Related Stoneware of Bennington*, Charles E. Tuttle, 1971.

8. Rushlight Club, *Early Lighting—A Pictorial Guide*, 1972.

9. Teleki, Gloria, *The Baskets of Rural America*, E.P. Dutton, 1975.

10. Webster, Donald, *Decorated Stone-ware of North America*, Charles E. Tuttle, 1971.

The Gould Collection

Listed among these suggested books are two volumes written by Mary Earle Gould, a pioneer collector of Americana. In the late 1960s Miss Gould, a native of Worcester, Massa-chusetts, donated her collection of early American woodenware and tin to the Hancock Shaker Village in Pittsfield, Massachusetts, and on May 31, 1984, a portion of the collection was sold at auction by Skinner's of Bolton, Massa-chusetts.

We read Gould's woodenware and tin and tin and toleware books each several times, and eventually wrote her a letter telling her how much we enjoyed her work. That letter began a long corre-spondence that resulted in Gould's writing a foreword for our first book more than twenty years ago.

We asked her several times if she had pieces from her collection that were for sale. She always indicated that nothing was ever going to be for sale. Probably to shut us up she put together some photographs of the collection, autographed the back of each one, and airmailed them to us.

As you will note from her pictures, she did not display what she had collected in room settings as most of us would do; instead, she turned the upstairs and attic of the home she shared with her mother into her museum.

Seventy-five chopping knives, twenty-five toddy stirrers, wooden bowls, and horse fly nets.

Trenchers, sugar bowls, apple drying basket, and early lighting equipment.

Boxes and slates, Gould's father's dental sign c. 1870, candlesticks.

Down the hall to the first collection of wooden boxes.

In the "long room" at the end of the hall were Shaker carriers, mortars and pestles, and cheese drainers.

17

Flatiron collection and candle mold collection.

Rare plate warmer and hanging potato baskets, tin ovens.

Butter scales, large basket for goose feathers, pig platter on a sawbuck table, rare butter prints.

Collections of rolling pins, washing equipment, and foot stoves.

19

Yokes, boxes, lighting, and horseshoer's box and tools.

Field Trips

Over the years we have visited each museum listed below several times and have been consistently impressed on each occasion. Collectors need a periodic respite from the road, and the opportunity to see great things in proper settings. We suggest visits to the Henry Ford Museum, Greenfield Village, Dearborn, Michigan; Old Sturbridge Village, Sturbridge, Massachusetts; the Shelburne Museum, Shelburne, Vermont; the Pennsylvania Farm Museum of Landis Valley, Lancaster, Pennsylvania; the Shaker Museum, Old Chatham, New York; and the Farmers' Museum, Cooperstown, New York. The Shelburne Museum, the Shaker Museum, and the Farmers' Museum are especially recommended for families with children.

Recommended Periodicals

Antique Markets Quarterly
P. O. Box 219
Western Springs, IL
60558-0219

This valuable quarterly, which comes out in January, April, July, and October, is published in regional editions, and lists antiques shows and markets in various sections of the nation. It provides dates, locations, number of dealers, and percentage of antiques and collectibles dealers at various flea markets. In the back of each edition is a listing of shows and markets classified by antique specialty.

Antique Review (formerly Ohio
Antiques Review)
12 East Stafford Avenue
Worthington, OH 43085

This monthly newspaper reviews antiques shows throughout mid-America and contains informative and in-depth articles about all aspects of Americana. Each issue is also filled with show, auction, and shop advertisements.

AntiqueWeek
P.O. Box 90
Knightstown, IN 46148

This weekly publication (formerly the Tri-State Trader) is found in several regional editions. AntiqueWeek is not devoted primarily to Americana but has interesting articles and numerous auction and show advertisements.

Illinois Antiques Gazette
4 S. Hill St.
Winchester, IL 62694

This newspaper is published eight times each year ($19.50) and focuses on antiques collecting in Illinois and east-ern Missouri. The advertisements for shows, auctions, malls, and markets and the informative articles make it an invaluable tool for antiquing in the Land of Lincoln.

New England Antiques Journal
Turley Publications
4 Church St.
Ware, MA 01082

This monthly publication focuses on antiques shows and shops primarily in the states of New Hampshire, Massachusetts, and Vermont. It also carries well-researched features on Americana and the antiques marketplace.

Sloan's Green Guide to Antiquing in
New England
The Antique Press
105 Charles St. #140 M,
Boston, MA 02114-2340

This publication gives more than 2500 descriptions of New England's best antiques shops, plus a show calendar, antiquing tours, profiles of 35 museum collections, and an index of dealer specialties. $18.95. (1-800-552-5632)

Antiques Shows and Markets

We have chosen to provide a listing of antiques show and markets promoters rather than individual events, because specific locations, dates, and times are highly subject to change.

If you are going to be in a geographical area served by any of the companies and promoters listed below, contact them directly for precise information about their events.

Midwest

3rd Sunday Market
P.O. Box 396
Bloomington, IL 61702-0396
(309) 452-7926

Kane County Flea Market, Inc.
P.O. Box 549
St. Charles, IL 60174
(708) 377-2252

J. Jordan Humberstone, Mgmt.
1510 N. Hoyne
Chicago, IL 60622-1804
(312) 227-4464

Allegan Antiques Market
2030 Blueberry Dr. N.N.
Grand Rapids, MI 49504

Ann Arbor Antiques Market
2393 Tessmer Rd.
Ann Arbor, MI 48103

Richard E. Kramer and Associates
427 Midvale Ave.
St. Louis, MO 63130

R. Bruce Knight
P.O. Box 533
Richfield, OH 45501

Burlington Antiques Show
P.O. Box 58367
Cincinnati, OH 45258

Heartland Shows
633 Lakengren Dr.
Eaton, OH 45320
(513) 456-5087

New England

Heart-O-The-Mart
Rte. 20
Brimfield, MA 01010
(413) 245-9556

J and J Promotions
Rt. 20, Auction Acres
Brimfield, MA 01010
(413) 245-3436

Farmington Antiques Weekend
Revival Promotions, Inc.
P.O. Box 388
Grafton, MA 01519
(508) 839-9735 or (1-800) 344-7469

New York and Pennsylvania

Sanford L. Smith and Associates
68 E. 7th St.
New York, NY 10003-8438

Jim Burke Antique Shows
3012 Miller Rd.
Washington Boro, PA 17582

Renninger's Promotions
27 Bensinger Dr.
Schuylkill Haven, PA 17972

Texas

Emma Lee Turney's Round Top
Antiques Fair
P.O. Box 821289
Houston, TX 77282-1289
(713) 493-5501

Washington

Dick Mattila
Western Antiques Exposition
P.O. Box 2113
Redmond, WA 98052
(206) 868-8943

Qualifying Examination

Before you are allowed to continue reading this edition of our book, we must determine that you are capable of absorbing the concepts and information herein. Please read the paragraph below and insert the proper word or phrase. Select your answer from the list of terms at the bottom of the page. You will find the correct answers on page 257.

If you miss more than one question we are not responsible for the consequences, but we will light a candle for you.

22

Mr. Smith packed his van to go to the antiques show. He decided to take ____ because he had sold almost all of his furniture to a ____ who had stopped by yesterday. He only had a ____ cupboard and a table with legs that had been ____ . He knew that ____ or ____ merchandise sold best at this show because the customers wanted collectibles, oak, and depression glass. He expected a big crowd because the promoter allowed ____ admissions for an extra $5.

a. picker   b. low end   c. late   d. pieced out   e. early bird
f. smalls   g. glazed

3 *Country Furniture*

When we made buying trips to Ohio and Pennsylvania in the late 1960s, country furniture was found in quantity in many antiques shops that specialized in Americana. At that time a potential buyer had relatively few worries about the finish of a piece under consideration. If the piece was painted, it was almost certainly legitimate because paint did not add a premium to the price tag as is the case today. There were probably many more collectors of refinished pine furniture than of examples with original surfaces. A pine cupboard that had been stripped, sanded, sealed, and waxed was usually more valuable than a similar one with its painted finish intact.

As the interest in original painted furniture slowly grew and prices increased, the level of sophistication required of the collector was also increased, because it now became profitable for a few less-than-scrupulous dealers to take the refinished pine cupboard out of the front window of the antiques shop and find someone to "reapply" its earlier painted finish.

The interest in Americana in its original condition has continued to flourish over the years. The demand for old painted furniture has far exceeded the supply, and reproductions are available through major American furniture manufacturers and local craftsmen.

There are a lot of individuals with varying levels of skill who can reproduce a nineteenth-century paint job on a twentieth-century piece of furniture. Much of the work looks like it was done with a broom, but some examples have fooled museum curators.

Therefore, when you purchase a piece of country furniture with a painted finish, make it a point to secure a receipt from the seller with a detailed description and a listing of any structural changes or alterations of the finish.

Paint

A major factor in evaluating a piece of country furniture and determining its value is the quality and degree of originality of its finish.

In the 1940s and 1950s most pieces of eighteenth- and nineteenth-century pine furniture were stripped, sanded, sealed, and waxed. Little thought was given to saving the original surface. Now, serious collectors are primarily interested in paint, and refinished country furniture generates minimal interest.

Terms

original paint: When the piece of furniture was initially painted, it was coated with its "original" paint. If the piece has been painted again at any point, it does *not* have its original paint. Relatively few examples of nineteenth-century furniture that are offered for sale today have not been overpainted or repainted one or more times. The value of a piece with its original paint is greater than a piece that has been overpainted.

old paint or overpaint: If a pine cupboard that dates from 1850 is described as carrying "old" blue paint, it means that the piece has been repainted, but it was done many years back, perhaps 50, 75, or 125 years ago. The fact that the paint is called old suggests that it wasn't done in the past 2 to 15 years.

late paint: Generally when a piece is described as being in "late" paint it is a veiled hint that it may still be wet. Late paint is almost a synonym for new paint. To some dealers a 1850s cupboard that was painted for the last time in the 1920s is covered with late paint. The late paint designation should stimulate some questions from the potential buyer.

"moved around" paint: A cupboard that has been stored in a basement, barn, or garage for several generations usually has lost some of its painted finish to the elements. It may still have some remnants of its original paint but not enough to keep. The alternatives are rather limited. The obvious one is to take the remaining paint down to the wood, clean it, sand it, seal it, wax it, and put it in the living room. A second alter-

Wood Types and Uses

Wood	How Wood Was Used	Where Found
ash	used in Windsor chair construction for pieces that had to be bent	Eastern U.S.
basswood	early Windsor chair seats, backboards on case pieces, drawer bottoms	U.S. and Canada
black cherry	arms of Boston rockers, tall clock cases, sometimes used in place of mahogany	Southern Appalachian Mountains
boxwood	inlay	West Indies
butternut	desks, cupboards, tables in Midwest in the nineteenth century	U.S.
chestnut	used in the 1600s and early 1700s for chests and table bases, later for unexposed framework in furniture	Eastern U.S.
ebony	inlay	India
hickory	spindles, chair arms, slats	U.S
mahogany	furniture, veneer	Haiti, Africa, Central and South America
maple	furniture, Shaker rocking chairs	Northeastern U.S.
pine	furniture that almost always was painted, basewood for American made veneered furniture, chair seats	U.S.
poplar	Midwestern furniture that was painted, drawer sides	U.S.
rosewood	inlay, furniture that was heavily carved	Brazil
spruce	drawer slides	Northeastern U.S.
sycamore	meatblocks, veneer, unexposed framework for furniture, drawer sides	U.S.
walnut	furniture that was usually not painted	U.S.
white oak	American furniture from the 1600s, chair spindles and slats, used in England for drawers and as a basewood for mahogany veneer	U.S.

native is to use paint remover to break up the existing old paint on the piece and turn it into a paste or semi-liquid form. This old paint is then moved or spread around to repaint the cupboard.

enhanced paint: A piece of furniture that has had its painted finish touched up with newly applied paint has been enhanced. This is often done to areas that have been repaired or replaced.

Wood

If one of your dreams is to be a national authority on wood, you have a reason to live. We have included a basic vocabulary and a chart that will answer all the questions the next time the subject is discussed.

Terms

bird's eye: Dips in the annual rings of the tree form a series of compressed circles that resemble a bird's eye.

burl: A wart-like growth on a tree trunk that is unusually hard and figured, used by cabinet makers for veneering, and by early Americans for bowls and kitchen implements.

crotch: Wood taken from a fork in the trunk of the tree or where large branches meet the tree trunk, which usually carries a heavily figured grain.

figures: Distorted patterns in wood caused by annual rings, burls, knots, or wavy grains. Examples of highly desirable figured wood are tiger maple and bird's-eye maple.

heartwood: Wood taken from the center of the tree trunk, which tends to be several shades darker in color than sapwood.

knot: The base of a limb on a tree.

sapwood: Wood taken from the outer portion of the tree.

veneer: Thin strips of semi-exotic wood (crotch grain, burl and other figured woods) glued to a softwood (usually pine) base for decorative effects.

Garth's Auctions

Garth's Auctions, Inc. of Delaware, Ohio is one of the nation's best-known sources for Americana sold at auction. Garth's offers detailed and heavily illustrated catalogs for each of their sales by mail and encourages telephone bidding. For $85 per year Garth's will forward a copy of all of its catalogs and a post-sale price list. For $65 collectors specializing in Americana will receive catalogs related to their interest and a post-sale price list for each auction.

All pieces of furniture shown here have been sold at a recent Garth's auction. Garth's *does* charge a 10% buyer's premium.

Information or a subscription can be secured by contacting:

Garth's Auctions Inc.
2690 Stratford Road, Box 369
Delaware, OH 43015
Telephone: (614) 362-4771
Fax: (614) 363-0164

Decorated blanket chest, poplar with reddish-brown vinegar graining over a yellow ground; original condition, dovetailed with bracket feet and till, $1100; horse pull-and push toy; some wear, but good overall condition; 27½" high × 27½" long, $500.

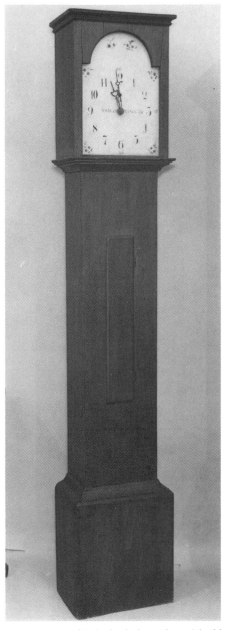

Country grandfather's clock, poplar with old dark cherry colored finish; wooden works with second hand and painted wooden face with worn original white paint, 79½" high. $1400

Country dry sink, pine with old worn blue repaint over grey, 52" wide. $350

Country jelly cupboard, butternut with old worn grey paint over earlier red, 33" wide × 59" high, **$900;** *wooden tricycle with cast-iron fittings and steel rims on wooden spoke wheels, 32½" high,* **$575.**

Decorated blanket chest, poplar with original brown graining over a white ground; turned feet, dovetailed case with till, 43" wide × 23" high, **$350**; horse pull-toy, stamped "Germany," 28" long × 30" high. **$425**

Country two-piece corner cupboard, pine with old worn green paint; probably a one-piece built-in cupboard originally, 52½" wide × 101½" high. **$1000**

Country one-piece corner cupboard, cherry with old mellow refinishing, double doors each with six panes of old glass, and cove-molded cornice, 80" high. **$1250**

Country one-piece wall cupboard, poplar cleaned down to old red, found in Murfreesboro, Tennessee. $1650

Country one-piece step-back wall cupboard, poplar with old brown repaint, $500; woven splint buttocks basket, wear and damage; $115.

Pie safe, pine with mellow refinishing; double doors each with three punched tins with blank repaint. $505

32

Small-grained blanket chest, pine and poplar with original red and black graining, turned feet, 34½" wide × 18" high, **$800;** *tin twenty-four tube candle mold with handle, 10" high,* **$250.**

Country water bench, poplar with old varnish finish, 48" wide × 15" deep. **$1000**

Painted immigrant's chest, pine with old worn green paint and black label "M. Nuninger,"
dovetailed with iron handles, 41½" long. **$125**

Country jelly cupboard, pine and poplar with old refinishing and traces of old steel comb graining, 52½" high, $600; hooked yarn mat, concentric rectangles with "Happy" in shades of pink and green, some wear, $275.

Settle bench, old black repaint with floral and foliage decoration; old repair, 82" long, **$375;**
"Chas. W. Wallace, Jewelry, Crockery" sign, 108" long, **$350.**

Country two-piece secretary, walnut with old refinishing, found in Ross County, Ohio. **$1000**

Country two-piece corner cupboard, refinished poplar and butternut. $1600

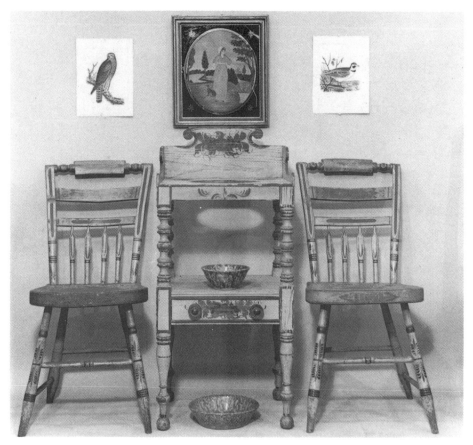

Set of six decorated plank-seat half-arrow-back side chairs, very worn old yellow paint with green striping and traces of stenciled detail, $750; decorated pine washstand, worn and flaking old yellow paint over a white undercoat, with brown striping and stenciled and freehand detail; $400.

Country Hepplewhite table, hardwood and pine with old worn refinishing, square tapered legs. $200

Country blanket chest with drawer, six-board construction, **$300;** *oval redware loaf pan, coggeled edge and yellow slip decoration,* **$425.**

Ladderback side chair, refinished hardwood, replaced woven splint seat, **$45;** *country Hepple-white school desk, pine with old worn mellow refinishing,* **$125.**

Country six-board blanket chest, dovetailed drawer, refinished pine, **$525;** *country ladderback side chair, varnish over traces of old red paint,* **$75.**

Country six-board blanket chest, refinished pine, till with lid, **$250**; *stave-constructed barrel-shaped butter churn with metal bands, old dark finish;* **$225**.

Country Chippendale high chest, poplar with old medium brown refinishing on all surfaces, replaced bracket feet, six overlapping dovetailed drawers and molded cornice. $1100

Early barrel-back corner cupboard, pine with old dark patina. $800

Country washstand, poplar with old cherry colored refinishing; replaced porcelain pulls. $350

43

Country blanket chest, refinished curly maple, dovetailed bracket feet, dovetailed case and dovetailed drawer, $1750; country Sheraton side chair with bamboo turnings, refinished and replaced rush seat, $55.

Country dry sink, pine and poplar with old worn refinishing, dovetailed drawer, 46" wide. **$450**

44

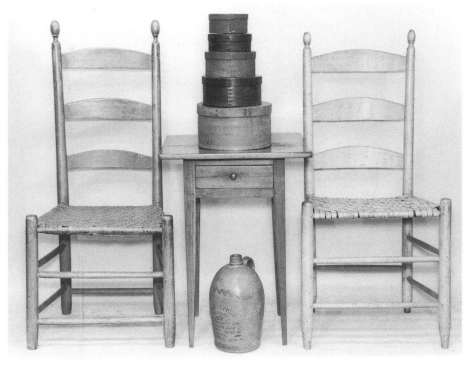

Ladderback side chair attributed to the Shakers, old worn salmon red over grey (at left), **$450;** *ladderback side chair, one side rung replaced and finials very slightly damaged,* **$650.**

Pennsylvania Chippendale high chest, cherry wood with old alligatored finish. **$10,000**

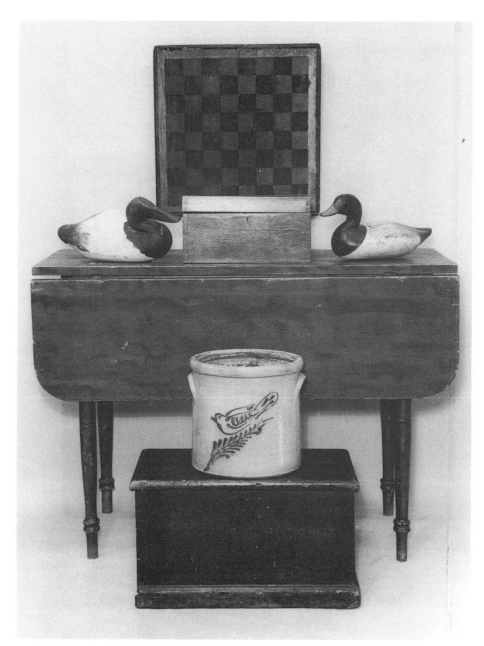

Country Sheraton Pembroke table, hardwood and pine with worn original red and black graining. **$175**

Country Hepplewhite stand, birch and pine with old refinishing, one dovetailed drawer, $225; bamboo Windsor armchair rocker, old dark worn finish with traces of white decoration on the crest and striping, $300.

Country two-piece wall cupboard, pine with old worn refinishing. **$2200**

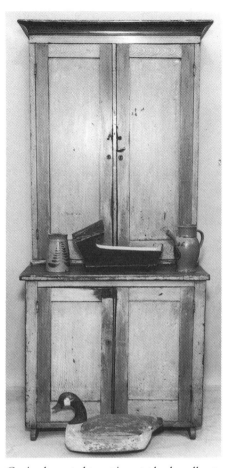

Grain-decorated two-piece stepback wall cupboard, pine with old worn brownish yellow graining, paneled ends and paneled doors with post office pigeon holes in top. **$900**

Continuous arm Windsor, cleaned down to old black, splayed base with turned legs, "H" stretcher. **$750**

Country Hepplewhite work table attributed to the Shakers, hardwood and poplar with old worn varnish finish. **$500**

Paint-decorated blanket chest, pine with old blue sponged paint, some old paint touch-up, and lid repainted, 38½" wide × 20" deep × 31½" high. **$2200**

Pennsylvania two-piece wall cupboard, pine and poplar with trace of brownish red paint and repainted black trim, bracket feet. $4250

Country one-piece step-back wall cupboard, cherry and poplar with mellow refinishing. $1100

Country two-piece plantation desk, refinished pine with traces of old red. $600

Country Sheraton Pembroke table, ash, poplar, and pine with old refinishing, **$250;** *Shaker ladderback side chair, mixture of hardwoods with old worn black paint,* **$75**.

Country cupboard, poplar with good old green paint over an earlier varnish finish, two dovetailed drawers, 79½" high, $610; late carved wooden cigar store Indian with polychrome paint, 72" high, $925.

Grain-painted side chair, c. 1860s. **$175–$225**

Rocking horse, original condition, c. late nineteenth century. **$3000–$4500**

Painted wheelbarrow. **$300–$400** *(Copake)*

Collection of black dolls. **$135–$200 (each)**

Child's toy chest of drawers, original painted finish, c. 1900. **$150–$175**

Extra-fine Schoenhut circus elephant, c. 1920. **$450–$550**

New England chair table, pine, original painted finish. **$1850–$2500**

Swing-handled basket, New England, nineteenth century. **$400–$500**

Painted basket, carved handle, New York state. **$800–$1250**

"Pure Raspberry Preserves" blue bucket, c. early 1900s. **$225–$300**

Rare red graniteware dairy pan, late nineteenth century. **$600–$800** *(Boggio collection)*

Pennsylvania butter crock. **$700–$800**

Ovoid jug, c. 1830s. **$335–$375**

Pennsylvania redware "master" inkwell, c. 1850. **$125–$175**

Cowden and Wilcos "man in the moon" jug. **$3500** *(Behr collection)*

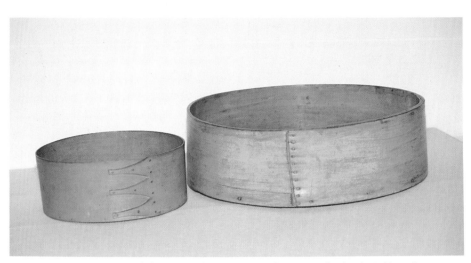

New England Shaker "spit" boxes, nineteenth century. **$750–$1250 each**

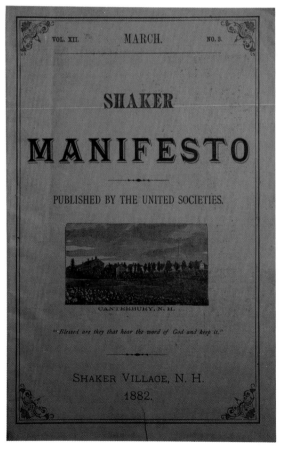

Shaker Manifesto for March 1882. **$55–$100**

Pennsylvania blanket chest, poplar with old worn red and brown two-tone finish, turned feet, **$325;** *hanging cupboard, walnut with old reddish finish,* **$850**.

Country stand, cherry with old worn refinishing, turned legs, three dovetailed drawers, **$495;** *bowback Windsor armchair, splayed base with turned legs,* **$550**.

Country two-piece plantation desk, refinished walnut and cherry, turned legs, scalloped apron, and fold-down writing surface in the base. **$850**

Decorated two-piece wall cupboard, poplar with original brown flame graining, 47" wide × 19½" deep × 84" high. **$3080**

Decorated settle bench, worn original grayish-yellow paint with brown and black striping. **$1375**

Set of five ladderback chairs, four side chairs and one arm chair, various hardwoods with reddish varnish refinishing. **$687.50**

Country one-piece corner cupboard, pine with stripped finish, 45" wide × 85½" high. **$1320**

Country one-piece corner cupboard, butternut with old worn refinishing, 43" wide × 72" high. **$1000**

Country two-piece wall cupboard, poplar with old dark red repaint, interior has modern yellow paint, 49½" wide × 81½" high. **$2090**

Country Hepplewhite work table, pine with old worn dark finish, square tapered legs, **$330;** *cast-iron windmill weight, rooster, traces of white paint, 20½" high,* **$990.**

Southern pie safe on stand, pine with old green repaint over earlier brown, North Carolina origin. **$1540**

Decorated blanket chest, poplar with old red and black graining with yellow trim over an earlier dark brown finish, 48½" wide, $1650; oil on canvas, primitive portrait of three children all wearing coral and gold jewelry, cleaned and restored, $2090.

Paint decorated apothecary chest, pine and poplar with mahogany top and old red flame graining over white, thirty dovetailed drawers in two sizes. **$4180**

Set of six bowback Windsor side chairs, old worn black repaint with yellow striping. **$5280**

Bamboo Windsor side chair, refinished, splayed legs, repairs in seat and one leg may have been replaced, $55; country drop leaf stand, refinished cherry with bird's eye veneer drawers, $715.

Country Sheraton stand, cherry with curly maple facade and top, old mellow refinishing, found in New York state. **$880**

Windsor bench, Philadelphia, old mellow refinishing, splayed base with bulbous turned legs and stretcher, 72½" long. **$5500**

Country Hepplewhite stand, walnut with old shiny varnish finish, square tapered legs, one dovetailed drawer, and removable two-board top, found in Ohio, **$385**; country Hepplewhite desk on frame, refinished butternut, square tapered legs with two dovetailed drawers in base, **$385**.

Country two-piece wall cupboard, refinished poplar, dovetailed, bracket feet, raised panel doors and three dovetailed doors in base, 48" wide. **$1430**

Country candlestand, refinished cherry, tripod base with spider legs, **$522.50;** *bowback bamboo Windsor arm chair, old red repaint over other colors, scrolled arms and seven-spindle back,* **$467.50.**

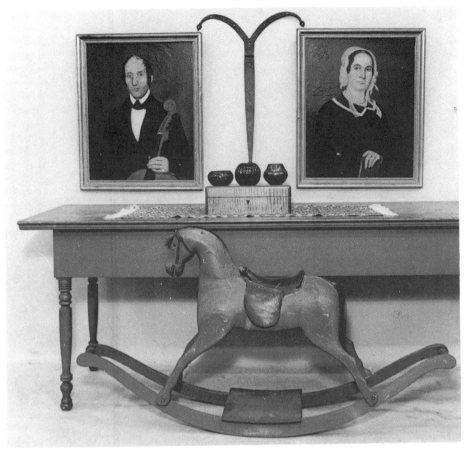

Country harvest table, pine with old brownish-gray repaint, turned legs, wide board apron and two-board top with applied edge molding, 105" long, $550; rocking horse, all wood with laminated construction and long curved rockers, old brown repaint over some repairs and metal patches, $660.

Country mule chest, refinished pine, six-board-type construction with two dovetailed drawers and two false drawers; base facade and lid molding are added or replaced, **$495**; tin churn, worn decal of flowers, rust damage, holes in bottom, **$55**.

Shaker cupboard, pine with old green paint, six dovetailed drawers below raised panel doors; interior has thirty pigeonholes and two shelves, 38½" wide × 18½" deep × 57½" high. **$4125**

Country pie safe, walnut with old dark worn finish, panels have circle and pinwheel design and are rusted and damaged; 39½" wide × 49½" high. **$990**

Country one-piece wall cupboard, pine with old refinishing, 27½" wide × 79" high. **$1320**

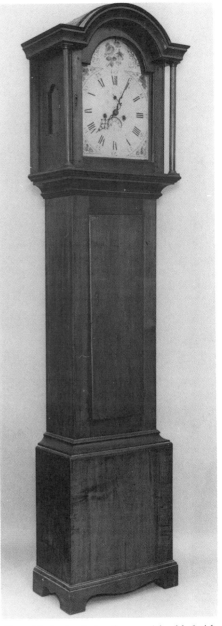

Grandfather's clock, cherry with old finish, bracket feet, 79½" high. **$4455**

Country Sheraton high chest, curly maple with old mellow refinishing, back boards replaced and top is a possible old replacement; 42¼" wide × 50½" high. **$1705**

Wicker Furniture: Pine Grove Antiques

American wicker furniture was almost a necessity in many late nineteenth-century and early twentieth-century backyards and on front porches.

The wicker furniture included in this section is from the collection and shop inventory of Pine Grove Antiques of Streator, Illinois. The business is operated by Ann Louise and Richard Ferguson, who specialize in wicker furniture that was made between 1900 and 1930. Mrs. Ferguson has been repairing and restoring antique wicker for more than 15 years.

The Fergusons
RR#3, 1365 Ridgewood Lane
Streator, Illinois 61364
Telephone: (815) 672-4963

Natural dark walnut-stained all reed sofa, three cushions, upholstered back with original fabric, 77" long × 22" deep, scalloped back and skirt, Ypsilanti Reed Furniture Company, c. early 1900s. **$750–$875**

All reed wicker desk with drawer and unusual bookends on bottom shelf, Heywood Wakefield Company. **$375–$450**

Similar high-back chairs made of twisted fibre with diamond design woven in the back, Ypsilanti Furniture Company, c. 1920s. **$225–$275 each**

Chaise longue, all reed with diamond designs, Heywood Wakefield Co., c. 1920s. **$600–$750**

Matched set of "Mr. and Mrs." chairs in all-reed construction, diamond designs on sides and in the skirt, Heywood Wakefield Company, c. 1920s. **$250–$285 each**

Twisted-fibre woven desk with lower shelf and arched design supports, wood inserts in top and lower shelf, c. early 1900s. **$185–$225**

Lloyd Loom wicker rocker with "set-in" arm rests, c. 1917–1930. **$225–$250**

Oval wood-top table with braid around the edge and twisted fibre wrapped legs, c. 1920s. **$250–$275**

Matched set of Lloyd Loom chair and rocker with design on back and turned wood frames, c. 1917–1930. **$225–$250 each**.

Lloyd Loom round table with unusual simu-
lated leather top, turned wood legs and braces,
c. 1917–1930. **$165**

Twisted-fibre and wood table, wrapped legs
and braid around the top and lower shelf, c.
1920. **$195**

Lloyd Loom sofa with "set-in" arm rests, c. 1917–1930. **$495**

Braided twisted-fibre square table with lower shelf and arched design supports, wood inserts in the top and lower shelf, c. early 1900s. $185–$225

Nice twisted-fibre rocker with diamond design and upholstered back, c. 1920. $250–$275

High-back twisted-fibre rocker with scalloped design on back, flared arms and open weave decoration in the center, c. 1920s. $250–$275

Unusual reed and oak side table, c. 1910. $100–$115

Three-piece matched set of twisted-fibre, "double stick" wicker, rocker and chairs, c. 1920s. **$800–$1000** *set*

White whatnot with three wooden shelves, c. 1890–1910. **$385–$450**

All twisted-fibre woven chair, closely woven seat and back with rolled arms. **$175–$200**

Twisted-fibre square box fernery with turned wood frame and metal liner, c. 1920. **$95–$115**

Seagrass flowerpot plant stand, c. 1900. **$75**

Twisted-fibre oblong fernery with turned wood frame and metal liner, c. 1920. **$125–$145**

Matched set twisted-fibre rocker and chair, closely woven back and arm tops with open weave design on the rest of the pieces, c. 1920s. **$250** *each*

Twisted-fibre and wood telephone stand, braid around the wood top with wrapped legs and supports, c. 1920. **$125**

Square back twisted fibre arm chair, c. 1920. **$195–$225**

Matched pair of twisted-fibre rockers, diamond designs on the back and skirt and teardrop designs under the arms, upholstered back, c. 1920s. **$200–$275** *each*

Small size twisted-fibre chaise longue, dia-mond design in back with lots of open weave; drop springs under the cushion, c. 1920s. **$450–$550**

Square-back rocker with square corner de-signs, twisted-fibre with diamond design in the back, c. 1920. **$250–$275**

Twisted-fibre oblong fernery with metal liner, turned wood frame with woven skirt, c. 1920s. **$135–$150**

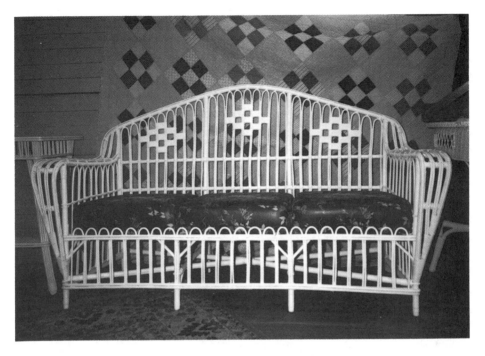

Reed "double stick" wicker matched three-piece set, three-cushion sofa, chair, and table with wood top and wood shelf, c. 1920s. **$1100–$1250**

4 *Kitchen and Hearth*

This chapter was prepared by Teri and Joe Dziadul; it illustrates items from their personal collection. The Dziaduls have been filling special requests for more than 20 years, and offer kitchen and hearth antiques for sale to collectors and dealers. The current list of items for sale may be obtained by sending $1.00 to the Dziaduls at 6 South George Washington Road, Enfield, CT 06082.

The swinging crane and the bubbling pot were central to the early New England home. The role of the fireplace has been extolled in poetry and prose, which dwells upon its charm and spiritual value in addition to its practical use. Longfellow, in a letter to a friend, Mr. J. O. Field, stated, "In one of the rooms was a tea kettle hanging on a crane in the fireplace—so begins a new household." Whittier, in praise of its warmth and cheer, wrote, "Between the andirons' straddling feet the mug of cider simmered slow, The apples sputtered in a row and close at hand, the basket stood with nuts from brown October's wood." Generations of today recite the old nursery rhyme, "Cross patch, draw the latch, sit by the fire and spin." The latchstring was the only means of opening the door from the outside. A cord with a peg tied to the end was attached to the latch, thrust through a hole above the latch and hung outside. By pulling the cord, the latch on the inside was lifted and the door could be opened. When privacy and security were desired, the string was pulled in and the door could not be opened from outside. An expression we hear today is derived from this old practice. "The latchstring is out for you" indicates that you would be welcome company.

There was a ready supply of hot water swinging on the crane, not only for cooking, but for soap making, candle dipping, and dying. Kettles held food for the morning meal, which often included hasty pudding. Prepared the night before, it was left in the kettle over the covered fire to be ready for morning and was eaten with milk, maple syrup, molasses, and butter when it was available. Breakfast, as the name implies, breaking the fast of the night, took place in the small hours of the morning by candlelight.

Baked beans with brown bread made of cornmeal became a Saturday custom. The beans waited in an earthenware pot—plump, shiny yellow eyes, molasses dark, their skins fairly bursting with goodness, the slashed salt pork peeking provocatively through the crusted surface. Before the beans stopped bubbling, they were laced with old-fashioned ketchup, when possible.

We are heirs of our ancestors, enamored of the lore of blackberry grunt, Indian pudding, and Vermont bean soup. Cranberry sauce conjures the imagination as well as the taste, recalling the reds of September. Steamed clams bring to mind the tang of salt spray on Nantucket Sound. Baked cod conveys the indefinable flavor of days long ago, and perpetuates the memory of the sea captains who sleep on the hill behind the silver-gray meetinghouses.

Many of us begin collecting quite by accident—finding and buying an object we admire. Our butterstamp collection came about in just this fashion. My husband, wishing to buy the perfect Christmas gift for me, returned to an antique shop where I had admired a footwarmer some time earlier. Much to his disappointment, the footwarmer had been sold. Searching for a meaningful compromise, he focused on a pair of buttermolds. As a result of that purchase, an ardent, consuming interest developed and the quest for butterstamps was launched.

Define your acquisition strategies. The optimum goal should be to find the very best of the category you love at your highest budget level. It is much better to acquire one good piece than several inferior ones. Acquiring the best of the past can enrich your present and future.

Questions and Answers

Veteran kitchen and hearth antiques dealer and collector Teri Dziadul of Enfield, Connecticut, has agreed to answer several questions for us about the turbulent state of the market for her specialty.

Q. How big a problem has the influx of woodenware and iron from countries outside the United States created for buyers and sellers of kitchen and hearth antiques?

A. It has created a considerable problem, particularly when vetted dealers with highest reputations exhibit imports and reproductions at shows. Collectors buy these items in good faith since they are given guaranteed statements of authenticity. More education is needed, and more articles should be published to inform collectors to *identify* these pieces.

Q. Is there any single category of kitchen and hearth antiques that has seen significant increases in price in the past year?

A. Woodenware.

Q. Is there any category that is currently underpriced?

A. Ironware—probably due to imports.

Q. If you were going to start a collection of kitchen and hearth-related antiques today, how would you begin?

A. I would purchase reference books, and join as many collector's groups as possible. These would provide invaluable information.

Q. What would you collect?

A. Apple parers, egg beaters, and iron hearth equipment.

Q. Are there some hints that you could give woodenware collectors to help them distinguish American pieces from European or Mexican?

A. Form (the shape of the item) and wide-grained woods contrasted with American pine, maple, and birch.

Cast-iron coffee roaster, hinged globe in frame, bail handle, sets on 3 legs. Globe has long handles which clamp together by the crank. Woods Patent—Roys & Wilcox Co. Pat. Apr. 17, 1849. Berlin, Conn. Harrington's Imp't. May 17, 1859. A wide price range exists. **$600—$975.**

Tin curfew—pierced design, Robacher Collection sale in Lancaster County, Pennsylvania (1987). These very early pieces were used to cover embers at the side of the fireplace, for safety and to shut off air. This preserved some embers for early morning when the fire was rekindled. The word curfew still remains today. In earlier days, a bell or whistle announced a certain time in the evening when all young people should be home and in bed. In England, during the reign of William the Conqueror, the bells were rung by law at seven in the evening so that all might cover the fire and extinguish the lights. **$875–$1000**

Cast-iron dutch oven, a large example—14" in diameter. These heavy iron pots have covers with deep rims to hold live coals, to get even heat for baking. It was set in the coals on its three legs, to bake corn pone or other food on the hearth. **$575–$675**

Cast-iron idleback, sometimes referred to as a tilter. This was very practical as it enabled the kettle to be tipped and poured while still on the crane. Embossed design on cover adds greater interest. **$525–$595**

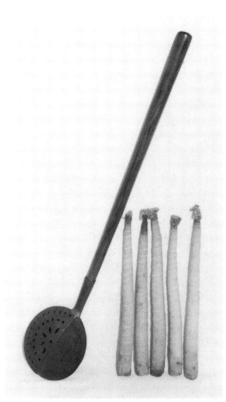

Tin tallow skimmer and tallow candles, un-usual pierced design in tin. The melted ani-mal fats (tallow) had to be skimmed of impurities before they could be used for mak-ing candles, **$275–$350;** *tallow candles,* **$85–$100** *each.*

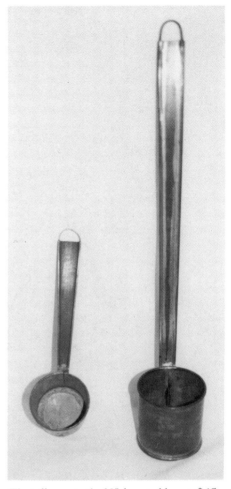

Tin tallow cup, tin 21" long toddy cup, **$65–$95** *each*

Higgins pie-carrying basket; made in Chesterfield, Massachusetts by generations of the Higgins family. Benjamin Higgins' work is definitely of the highest quality and design in American basketry. One of our country's great basketmakers, he stated his case well: "I am the world's finest basketmaker or the maker of the world's finest basket—whichever you prefer. I only make one quality—the best." **$350–$395**

85

Double footwarmer—pierced hearts design, tin box in wood frame with wire carrying handle. Opening in tin door for insertion of tin pan which contains hot coals for use in buggy, sleigh, or in unheated churches. This enabled 2 people to utilize footwarmer. **$575–$675**

Oval Nantucket sewing basket, only 7¼" long by 5" wide, narrow oak ribs tapered at bottom and chamfered slightly at the sides, tiny copper nails put in such a way they scarcely show. An example of very painstaking work, **$750–$850**.

Maltese Cross butter molds; the name is derived from the unfolded mold. Long thought to be Swiss in origin, consensus now favors Austria as country of origin. 3" high mold, **$245–$275;** *1¾" high mold,* **$185–$200**.

Hearth accessories: cast iron bowl, **$110–$125;** *tin apple roaster,* **$475–$525;** *pewter teapot, Morey & Ober,* **$325–$375;** *iron standing crane,* **$795–$895.** *An irreverent, amusing adaptation of Mother Goose Rhymes:*

> "Doctor Foster found he'd lost a
> Rare old wrought-iron crane
> By being too thrifty and bidding one-fifty,
> He never will do it again!"

Mother Goose for Antique Collectors

*Hearth accessories: standing crane, **$795–$895**; kettle tilter, **$650–$750**; dutch oven w/ handle—marked Fair Day & D. Klyne Knoxville, Tennessee—13" diameter. The brick oven is often erroneously called a dutch oven, **$525–$625**; small tin reflector oven (the larger versions are called tin kitchens). The open part is intended to face the fire. A door swings open to enable the cook to inspect or baste the meat. A spit runs through the center of the oven to accommodate the skewers when attaching roast. Small ovens are more scarce. **$325–$395**; Cast Iron porringer, marked Bellevue, **$150–$200**.*

*Higgins basket, ash splint, staves and handle, pine bottom. **$375–400***

Tin flour scoop, is an advertising piece from Pillsbury and marked so, handle unscrews for paper with recipes from company, $65–$75; blue onion flour canister in excellent condition, $125–$150.

Fowl butterstamps and mold: quail butterstamp, 2" diameter, intricate carving, $300–$350; crane stalking prey butterstamp, $750–$850; pea fowl buttermold, rare subject, $795–$895. Grandma Moses once remarked that as a farm wife she sold her printed home-churned butter at nearly twice the price of other butter to the same market.

Factory-made buttermolds: half-pound mold, geometric print, $25–$35; Reid's Buttermold, offered in Montgomery Ward's 1895 catalog, 1 lb. size, $45–$65.

Freestanding two-piece chick buttermold in shipping box, from Beatrice Creamery Co., Chicago, Illinois, makers of Meadow Gold Butter. A complimentary gift by the manufacturer to consumer with instructions for use of mold. $125–$150

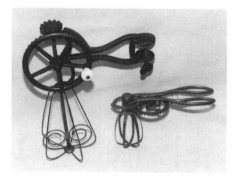

Iron clamp-on beater, cast frame, wire beaters, porcelain knob; very rare, $600–$650; scissors-type eggbeater, marked "Pat. No. 1," referred to as the Jaquette, patented by Harry Jaquette of Philadelphia, Pennsylvania, c. 1893, $585–$650.

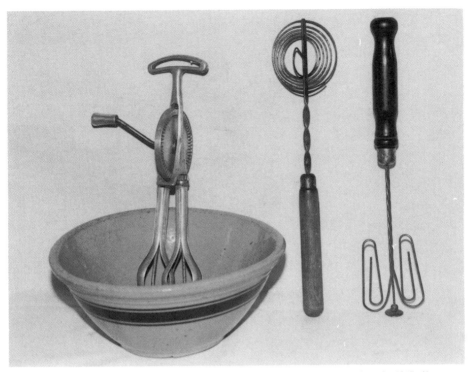

Yellowware bowl and beating devices: yellowware bowl with vivid brown bands, 9½" diameter, **$45–$55;** *instant whip aluminum beater, patented April 20, 1920,* **$20–$25;** *spiral whipper, Archimedes' principle action,* **$55–$65;** *A & J Mfg. Co. beater, patented October, 1907,* **$75–$85**.

Mayonnaise mixer, S & S No. 1, or Scientific and Sanitary; S & S forms casting design of gear wheel; glass lid with oil funnel built in. This was patented Sept. 2, 1913. **$378–$400**

*Food chopper, 6 steel blades with wood handle, scarce, **$145–$175**; wood chopping bowl, **$85–$95**.*

*Wood rolling pins: double-barred handle for extra strength and better grip, late eighteenth-century characteristics, **$350–$395**; springerle rolling pin, springerle (lively little horse) is a traditional cookie for St. Nicholas Day, December 6; rolling pin is rolled over dough to make the designs. Squirrels, rooster, and deer are more desirable subjects than flowers and leaves; mid-nineteenth century, **$275–$300**.*

Wood rolling pin and pastry board, rare framed rolling pin with unusual perpendicular handle, eighteenth-century, $400–$450; pastry board, $95–$110.

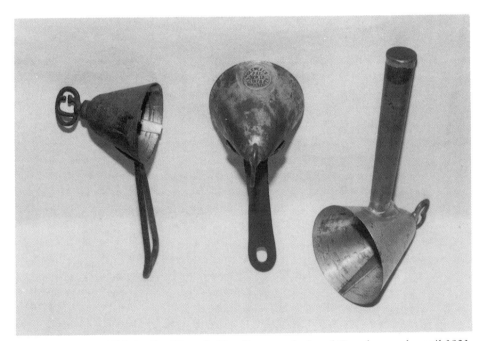

Ice cream dishes: Gilchrist Co., Newark, New Jersey, steel, tinned G on key, made until 1931, $30–$35; key-operated conical disher, round company seal on front of cone, Clewell's Pat. November 12, 1878, V. Clad Maker, $70–$80; key-operated conical disher, tubular tin handle, round seal on end of handle marked "Clewell's V. Clad Maker, Pat. November 12, 1878," stamped in handle "117–119 So. 11th St. Phila. Pa.," $70–$80.

Wood spice box with 8 containers, Mauchline transfer designs around container and one on cover; a scarce version. **$395–$425**.

Wood bread board, Give Us This Day Our Daily Bread, oak leaves and acorns carved around border. This board has mustard yellow paint remnants on border, age crack, **$125–$145**; bread knife, **$85–$95**.

Oval wood bread board, not as common as round boards, **$145–$175**.

Wood butter dishes, glass liners, individual butter pat dish, blue opaline liner, deep carving, **$90–$100**; butter dish, blue opaline liner, **$75–$95**; butter knife, **$75–$85**; individual butter pat dish, green hobnail liner, **$85–$95**.

94

Wood butter dishes and knives: standard size butter dish, $90–$100; rare large size butter dish, 9" diameter, extravagantly carved, blue opaline liner, $175–$195; butter knife, EPNS blade, $75–$85; butter knife, steel blade, $85–$95.

Architectural elements: acorn finial, brown varnish finish, $50–$75; artichoke, blue-green paint, base in poor condition, $75–$85; acorn, gilt finish, $95–$125.

Brass trivet, rare heart in hand design, c. 1840. $325–$375.

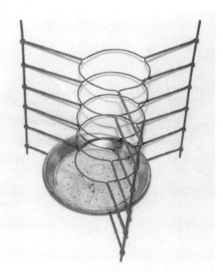

Ice cream scoops: United Products Co., Chelsea, Massachusetts, this shape was used for banana splits and is a rare form, $600–$700; Q & E Specialty Co., Erie, Pennsylvania, Patented 1908, $175–$195; Clipper, F.S. Co., Troy, New York, #5 on thumb lever. Conical portion has unusual crease extension. Scarce, $225–$250. Analysis of patent records between 1878 and 1940 indicated that the nomenclature preferred disher *to "dipper";* scoop *was hardly used. Scoop became common in present day usage probably because it is concise.*

Wire pie rack, triangular form with 15½" angle spread. Scarce version. $150–$175

Wire baker display tray, $55–$75.

Toby pepperpots: Staffordshire pottery and silver lustre, c. 1840–1860. This decorative ware was coated with a thin film of silver. Platinum, first available in the 1790s, yielded silver for this application. **$150–$195**

Large ginger jars: Canton, China, c. 1785–1825. The vast Chinese empire attracted enterprising seamen to make perilous voyages to the East in return for wealth and adventure. The porcelain brought back to the West is now known as Chinese export. **$250–$395**.

French delft platter, 16" long. Professional restoration to cover a hairline crack. **$550–$650**

French delft plate and charger, 10" diameter plate, edges of plate are warped, **$225–$250;** *12" diameter charger,* **$650–$750**.

Mocha butter crock and mug, butter crock, 4½" diameter, blue seaweed pattern, $325–$375; mug, black and olive seaweed pattern, $275–$300.

Tin flour sifter, blue onion flour canister: tin paddles push out the sifted flour, patent stamp, "Earnshaw's Patent July 25, 1866." A combination scoop and sifter, $95–$145; flour canister in fine condition, $100–$125.

Rouen, France delft platter, 13¼" long, c. 1760. This pottery utilizes a redware base with a gray crackle glaze body and blue decoration. Shards of this French delft were found in excavations at Williamsburg. **$650–$750**

Boston stoneware jug, tan and ochre color glaze, incised rings around neck and base, ovoid form. **$300–$350**

Pair of small advertising jugs, cream and brown glaze, 7" high. **$100–$125**

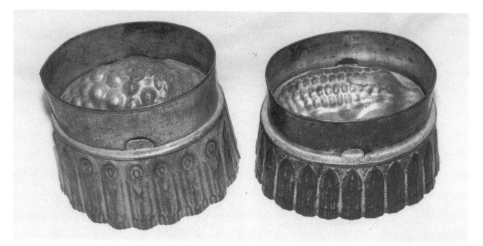

Tin pudding molds, grapes and ear of corn design: when time permitted, housewives took pride in presenting attractive desserts. **$75–$85**

Tin cup, sugar storage box, cream can, cup, **$12–$15;** *sugar box, wood grips fold down to permit removal of wood cover. Braided tape secured to inner recessed edge for air-tight storage,* **$145–$175;** *cream can with wood stopper,* **$30–$35.**

Tin rattles: child's rattle, 5¼" long, **$50–$55;** *10th Wedding Anniversary rattle, 7¼" high, 6" diameter, 6" long handle. Punched inscription on side reads as follows: For Boys Only—December 8th, 1872,* **$550–$600.**

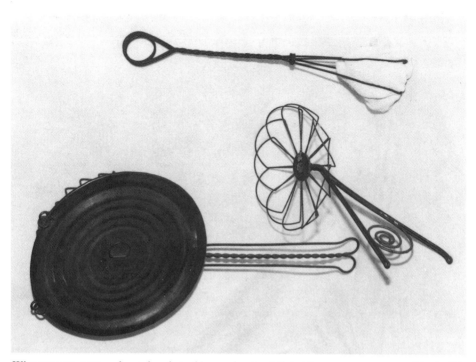

Wire popcorn popper, lamp bracket, chimney lamp, cloth holder, popcorn popper with tin lid, **$40–$45;** *lamp bracket, wire base revolves,* **$30–$35;** *cloth holder to clean soot from inside of glass lamp chimneys,* **$20–$25.**

Tin three-tube candlemolds: scalloped top and base. Scalloped ends command higher prices, **$250–$275;** *scalloped top, tubes are splayed into a square bottom.* **$135–$175**

Milliner's Head Model, wood glove forms, papier mache construction, **$950–$1100;** *pair of glove forms, moveable sections, size 6½,* **$250–$275.**

Brass and tin graters: large graters were utilized for many purposes from horseradish and cucumbers to cheese. All brass grater on iron frame, $125–$145; all tin grater on wire frame, punched decoration in tin, which enhances its value, $125–$150; tin bread grater, c. 1890, $85–$100.

Lemon reamers: all wood, hand carved, $125–$145; corrugated head, finely turned handle, $125–$150; two folded tin sections fit into turned handle. A scarce example, $125–$150. To prevent scurvy, sailors took these hand-held reamers on long sea voyages. Hence, they came to be known as "limies."

Variations of pie crimpers: All wood, brass, pewter, and porcelain wheels. $85–$145

Cracker Prickers: Wood handle, iron prongs.
$70–$85:. *All wire,* **$50–$65.**

Blue onion ware: butter dish, marked Meissen, **$145–$165;** *sauce boat, Meissen,* **$75–$85;** *funnel, only 3" diameter,* **$45–$50;** *Escargot plate, Collin, Meissen,* **$65–$75.**

Blue onion ware: gravy boat and saucer, **$85–$95;** *Pitcher, Villeroy & Boch, Germany,* **$85–$95;** *uncommon potato masher,* **$125–$145.**

Bee skep: rye coil was used for centuries since it was cheaper than wood, warmer in cold weather, and cooler in warm weather. **$250–$300**

Tin grater and wood bowl, uncommon form with projecting handle on grater, hanging ring, **$65–$75**; *wood chopping bowl,* **$85–$95**.

Blue onion canisters: nutmeg and clove spice jars, $65–$75; *prune jar,* $125–$140.

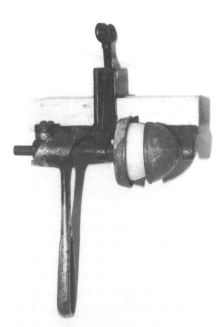

Pie Lifter, steel and wood handle. Spring tension steel grips the edge of a pie for removal from oven. **$45–$55**

Cast-iron lemon squeezer; marked "The Leader, Leader Mfg. Co. Hartford, CT USA." Patented March 12, 1901, **$145–$175.**

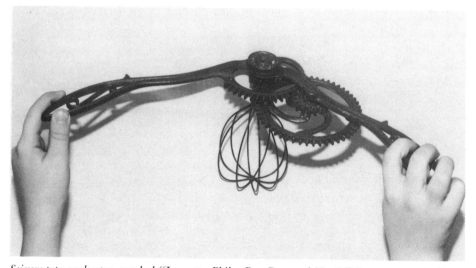

Scissors-type eggbeater, marked "Jaquette, Phila, Pa., Patented No. 3." Patent papers indicate this was invented by Harry Jaquette, Nov. 28, 1893. In one paragraph, he states, "The object of my invention is to so construct an implement for beating or stirring materials in performing difficult culinary operations that said implement can be conveniently handled and the maximum amount of power exerted in order to cause the rotation, first in one direction and then in the opposite direction, of the beating or stirring device." A scarce example, **$600–$695.**

106

Mechanical nutmeg graters: tin, marked "The Little Miller," w/original card of instructions, $375–$475; tin, wood, paper label, Brown & Hasler, rotary nutmeg grater, Lynn, Massachusetts, $895–$1000; all wood with tin grating surface, very scarce version in all wood frame, $450–$550.

Glass cake stand with covered dome lid, $300–$350.

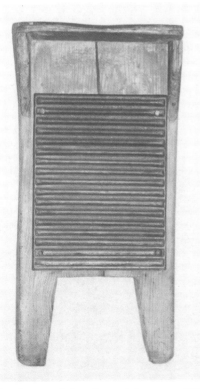

Cast iron wash board, wood frame, c. 1850. $175–$200

Doris Stauble arrangement, in old blue firken with wax fruit and old millinery filler. $275–$325

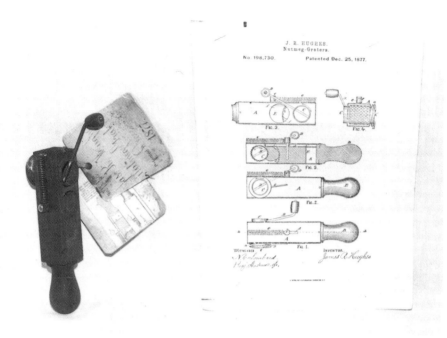

Mechanical nutmeg grater with original patent model papers, J. R. Hughes, Saugus, Massachusetts, Patented December 25, 1877. One paragraph in the patent papers reads as follows: "My invention relates to that class of graters in which the grating surface is formed upon the periphery of a cylinder adapted to revolve past the side of the nutmeg, and by constant and successive action of its teeth thereon reduce it to a fine powder." The accompanying original patent model papers dramatically increase the value of this version. **$595–$695**

Hooked rug, folk art, brown dog with salmon ball in mouth on dark gray background with red clover motifs in each corner. **$450–$500**

Apple parer on painted board; this version appears in 3 sizes—6", 7", or 8" large gear wheel. Red painted wood base. All known versions are of Maine origin, but maker remains elusive, c. 1850, scarce. **$450–$550**

Wax fruit in wire basket, wire basket, **$95–$125;** *wax fruit,* **$10–$15** *each.*

Painted hanging wall cupboard, painted in original blue with interior shelves. **$550–$650**

Syrup pitcher and cruet, clear glass pitcher with applied amber handle, etched fern fronds, pewter lid with dolphin thumb flip. Patented July, 1872, **$145–$165;** *cranberry glass cruet, blown clear stopper, applied clear handle.* **$175–$195**

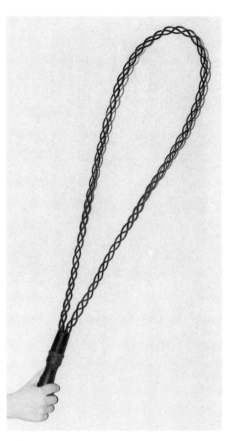

Rug beater, wood handle, tin ferrule, braided wire. Beaters were once part of an annual rite of spring cleaning. Rugs were taken outdoors, hung over clotheslines, and beaten to remove dust and soot produced from stoves and oil lamps. **$30–$35**

Apple parer mounted on board; a separate knife would have been held against the apple as the handle was cranked. Wrought iron, late eighteenth century. **$200–$295**

Scutching knife, cranberry scoop, cabbage slaw board: Rosemaled wooden knife used to beat the harvested flax to free the flax from the coarse plant slivers, dated 1832, $300–$400; cranberry scoop for harvesting berries in the bog, all wood teeth, wire front, $300–$350; slaw cutter with heart cutout. An authentic heart cutout is much desired. Beware recently carved hearts in otherwise plain cutters, edges will feel rough to the touch. $250–$295

Miniature baskets in blue wall cupboard: Maine Indian candy basket, $40–$45; Maine Indian Easter candy basket, old candy Easter Eggs intact, $50–$60; Shaker sewing basket with pincushion and wax strawberry, $275–$350; Maine Indian curlicue basket, $65–$75; signed Nantucket basket, very scarce, $350–$400; narrow splint baskets, $30–$35.

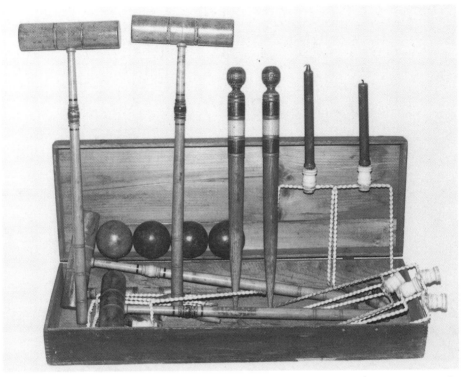

Croquet set with candle sockets: a very scarce set with twisted wire wickets, painted white; balls, mallets and stakes in colorful paints. Original box. **$1200–$1500**

Tasha Tudor water color painting, Christmas street vendors scene with snow sculpture. **$4000–$5000**

5 *Decorated Stoneware*

Evaluating Stoneware

A piece of stoneware is normally evaluated on the basis of its decoration, condition, color, form, and maker's mark. An extremely desirable example would have an elaborately executed deer on a pristine four-gallon crock surrounded by a fence, trees, and vegetation. The color of the decoration would be a deep cobalt blue. Stamped into the front of the crock would be a manufacturer's mark that reads "J. & E. Norton, Bennington, Vt." Since this is a dream, let's assume that we found the crock at the garage sale of a neighbor you detest, for four dollars.

An undecorated three-gallon crock or jug is as likely to be purchased at a yard sale in Ohio as at a flea market at the Rose Bowl. If it is an unmarked, molded example from the late nineteenth century, it will generate little interest and probably sell for $15–$20. Regardless, it is an extremely common collectible that is not difficult to locate.

A three-gallon jug with a hastily executed cobalt flower is more desirable and a touch more challenging to locate than the undecorated jug, but it still falls within the common range. Ten years down the road this statement probably will not be true.

A simple cobalt house with no detail is certainly an uncommon piece of stoneware that would take some work to locate. It approaches "rare" but is less difficult to uncover than a cobalt house with architectural detail, a fence, ground cover, and trees. This piece would rate a strong "rare."

A crock, churn, or jug with the scene of a baseball game, players, crowd, and additional details would be off the rarity chart and probably bring well into five figures, if an example were

One of the keys to securing an approximate date for a piece of stoneware is to carefully study its shape. This jug is pear-shaped or ovoid in form, and dates from the 1830 to 1840 period. Later nineteenth-century pieces are almost cylindrical in shape.

A stoneware collector's dream is to find a shelf in the basement of a home in some New York state hamlet that is stocked with elaborately cobalt decorated crocks, jars, and jugs. This grouping includes slip-trailed birds, animals, and a house with sheltering palm trees.

116

The desirability of this churn is enhanced by the addition of the "1896" date. Dated pieces of stoneware are not rare but would certainly fall within the "uncommon" category.

The human face within the starburst on the six gallon churn makes it an extremely rare piece of decorated stoneware. Cobalt faces or human figures were executed on nineteenth-century stoneware primarily by special order or as gifts made by the pottery's decorators.

The flower decoration on this four-gallon crock was also done with a slip cup or slip trailer.

ever found without severe structural damage.

If we took a nineteenth-century four-gallon crock and evaluated it, we would look at numerous variables. As noted above, decoration, color, mark, and condition would be essential considerations. To secure some insight into degree of rarity, let's take the four-gallon crock and examine it with a variety of cobalt decorations.

Common (swirls or lines):

1. Could be found in a local antiques shop or mall.
2. Several could be found at a farm sale or auction.

117

3. Commonly found in general line antiques shops.
4. There will be one on the front porch of a house in the subdivision down by the hardware store.

Uncommon (simple bird):

1. Probably could be found at an antiques show that emphasizes country merchandise.
2. Several would be in the inventory of stoneware dealers.
3. Occasionally found in general line shops or malls (overpriced).
4. Found at auctions where the primary emphasis is on stoneware.

Rare (deer and trees):

1. Could be found in the inventory of a major stoneware dealer.
2. Several examples typically can be found among dealer offerings at

The "chicken pecking corn" decoration is typically found on crocks rather than jugs. This chicken was done with a slip cup rather than a brush. The slip cup leaves a raised trail of cobalt on the surface of the stoneware.

Decorated utility pieces like butter pails and pitchers are uncommon. This cobalt flower was hastily drawn with a slip cup.

A piece of this quality can acquire rim chips and hairline cracks and still maintain significant value. A five-gallon crock with a simple flower or cobalt swirl loses most of its worth, and almost all of its desirability to collectors, with even minor chips or cracks.

It is also possible to date a piece of stoneware by its maker's mark. The J. Norton and Co., Bennington, Vermont, mark was in use between 1859 and 1861.

Pails of this type were used for pancake batter and only occasionally were decorated. This Pennsylvania example was decorated with a brush.

The slip-trailed tree stands alone on the New York state crock.

The J. and E. Norton mark was in use between 1850 and 1859.

major country-Americana oriented antiques shows.

3. Found at auctions where the focus is on "high end" decorated stoneware.

Extremely rare (people in a scene):

1. At a major Americana show in an urban setting one or two examples *might* be found.
2. Offered by a collector or dealer due to personal circumstances or due to the dissolution of a major collection.
3. Major stoneware dealers offer 2 or 3 examples each year for sale or on consignment from collectors.
4. Found at an auction where the focus is on that specific piece of stoneware.
5. A previously unknown piece may show up at a rural auction (buying a lottery ticket is a better investment of time).

STONEWARE RARITY CHART

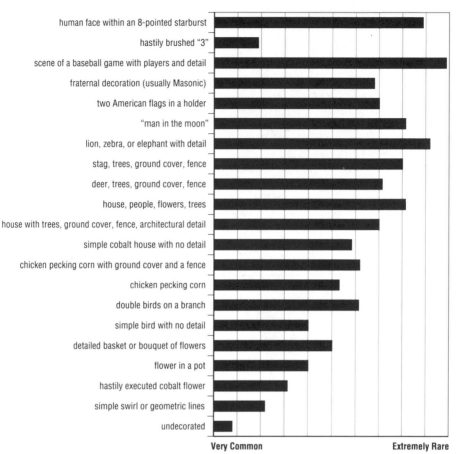

	Very Common ← → Extremely Rare
human face within an 8-pointed starburst	
hastily brushed "3"	
scene of a baseball game with players and detail	
fraternal decoration (usually Masonic)	
two American flags in a holder	
"man in the moon"	
lion, zebra, or elephant with detail	
stag, trees, ground cover, fence	
deer, trees, ground cover, fence	
house, people, flowers, trees	
house with trees, ground cover, fence, architectural detail	
simple cobalt house with no detail	
chicken pecking corn with ground cover and a fence	
chicken pecking corn	
double birds on a branch	
simple bird with no detail	
detailed basket or bouquet of flowers	
flower in a pot	
hastily executed cobalt flower	
simple swirl or geometric lines	
undecorated	

Very Common   **Extremely Rare**

Stoneware Video Tape

Over the past several years we have had more telephone calls and letters with questions about decorated stoneware than any other topic we have touched upon in our books.

We have put together an instructional video tape that covers all aspects of collecting and evaluating decorated stoneware. A copy can be secured for $21.95 (postpaid) by writing:

Don and Carol Raycraft
RR #8
Normal, IL 61761

C.W. Braun was in operation in Buffalo, New York in the 1860s.

120

Questions and Answers

Longtime stoneware dealers Bruce and Vicki Waasdorp of Clarence, New York, were gracious enough to answer several questions for us about the current state of the market for nineteenth-century decorated stoneware pottery.

Q. Over the past 12 months what changes have you noted in the market for decorated stoneware?

A. Prices and demand have been relatively steady to slightly down. I believe this is a reflection of the recessionary economy and the decrease of available discretionary income.

Q. Is there an aspect of the stoneware market that you feel is currently overpriced?

A. Only the occasional excessive auction price brought about by determined collectors filling specific collection voids.

Q. Underpriced?

A. The gap between good representative middle stoneware (i.e. $300–$1500), and the best of the category has widened, with great pieces commanding 10 times that and more. In that sense, the middle level is underpriced.

Q. If you were starting a collection of stoneware today, where would you begin?

A. Begin with what you like and the best you can afford. This is true for any category.

Q. If you were buying stoneware as a long term investment, what pieces would have the most interest for you?

A. The best examples seem to appreciate the fastest. Antiques strictly as investment are risky. I tell our customers to enjoy their collections, and if they appreciate considerably in value it is only a plus.

Q. How important in evaluating a piece of decorated stoneware are the following factors?

A. *Condition*: Good condition is more important on lesser pieces. With unique or rare designs, it does not play as much a part. Damage does affect price; the values we have shown in this guide assume damage-free condition.
Mark: Rare or short-time-period marks will generally bring a premium. Also, pieces from some factories are more desirable because their designs are known to be more elaborate.

The value of this slip-trailed reclining deer was increased with the addition of the pine trees, ground cover, and fence. If the decorator had taken another two seconds and placed a hunter in the scene, the line of potential buyers would stretch around the block.

Decoration: Probably the #1 factor in price consideration, since the "art work" is what you are buying.

Form: The same decorations found on common forms, that is crocks and jugs, will bring more money if found on the less commonly made forms like pitchers, bowls, or miniatures.

Q. Are reproductions a major problem for collectors today?

A. Not yet. All reputable contemporary potters mark their work. Also, new stoneware has a different "ring" to it. A cheap price is always a clue that some-thing is suspect. Always buy from reputable dealers and you won't be deceived.

Q. Are there two or three stoneware books that should be in every collector's library?

A. 1. *Potters and Potteries of New York State*, William Ketchum Jr., Syracuse University Press.

2. *American Stoneware*, William Ketchum Jr., Henry Holt & Co.

3. *Decorated Stoneware Pottery of North America*, Donald Webster, Tuttle Company.

The Waasdorp Collection

Vicki and Bruce Waasdorp are antiques dealers who specialize in nineteenth-century Americana and accessories in original condition. They have a special interest in decorated stoneware pottery and publish a semi-annual illustrated price list of stoneware that they have for sale.

Much of their business is conducted, by mail, with novice and advanced collectors and antiques dealers from throughout the United States. The stoneware photographs that follow are from the Waasdorp collection. Information may be secured by contacting:

Vicki and Bruce Waasdorp
10931 Main Street
Clarence, New York 14031
Telephone: (716) 759-2361

"Jordan" one-gallon ovoid jug, **$150–$200;** *"Lyons" one-gallon jug,* **$150–$200;** *West Troy, New York Pottery one-gallon jug,* **$400–$500.**

Burger and Lang, Rochester, New York, two-gallon crock, flower decoration, **$200–$300;** *J. Fisher, Lyons, New York, two-gallon dragonfly decoration, crock.*

New York Stoneware Co., Ft. Edward, New York, two-gallon crock, bird decoration, **$350–$450**; F. T. Wright and Son, Taunton, Massachusetts, stenciled blue crock, tiger design, **$300–$400**.

West Troy Pottery, three-gallon jug; great chicken pecking corn, cobalt decoration. **$1200–$1500**

E. and L.P. Norton, Bennington, Vermont, four-quart batter pail, **$400–$500**; White's Utica, New York, one-gallon jug, pine tree decoration, **$150–$200**.

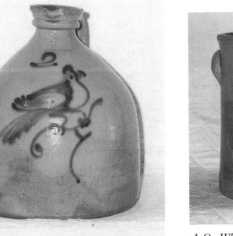

A.O. Whitmore, Havana, New York, four-gallon crock with rare house decoration. **$1800–$2300**

Uncommon batter jug with pouring spout, unsigned with bird decoration. **$500–$600**

123

Unsigned ½-gallon pitcher, $400–$500; ½-gallon unsigned preserve jar, $300–$400; "Peep-O-Day" chicken feeder, $50–$75.

Frank B. Norton, Worcester, Massachusetts, two-gallon jug with deep blue dove decoration, $700–$900; Bosworth, Hartford, two-gallon jug, decorated, dated 1886, $450–$550.

One-gallon advertising jug in blue script, $150–$200; one-gallon jug, ovoid, "1830" in blue, $300–$400.

J. and E. Norton, Bennington, Vermont, two-gallon pitcher, rare design and size, repaired and restored, $350–$450; unsigned two-gallon pitcher, rare size, $650–$750.

Two matching stenciled advertising crocks. $150–$200 each

F. B. Norton, Worcester, Massachusetts, 1½-gallon cake crock, rare size, $450–$550; unsigned one-gallon bird crock, $300–$400.

Lyons, New York, two-gallon jug, $150–$200; John Burger, Rochester, New York, two-gallon jug, $275–$375.

124

"Mead Ohio," two-gallon ovoid-shaped jug.
$300–$400

P. Mugler, Buffalo, New York, two-gallon jug, $450–$550; J. Burger Jr., Rochester, New York, $250–$350.

Selection of molded stoneware, c. 1900, White's Utica Pottery; small stein, $300–$400; canteen, $650–$750; large stein, $500–$600.

C.W. Braun, Buffalo, New York, two-gallon crock with unique tree design. $1500 and up

Group of New York state signed advertising script jugs. $150–$250 each

C. Hart, Sherbourne, New York, two-gallon crock with thick blue decoration. $325–$425

125

Ft. Edward Pottery Co. two-gallon jar with lid, $450–$550; "Lyons," New York, two-gallon jar with lid, $450–$550.

C.W. Braun, Buffalo, New York, four-gallon crock, abstract flower. $350–$450

W.H. Farrar, Geddes, New York, four-gallon preserve jar, detailed flowers. $350–$450

Two early signed Buffalo, New York, ovoid jugs, c. 1840. $450–$550 each

J. Norton, Bennington, Vermont, five-gallon jug, large dark blue decoration, $550–$650; uncommon four-gallon store-marked jug with floral decoration, $470–$575.

J. Fisher, Lyons, New York, two-gallon crock. $100–$150

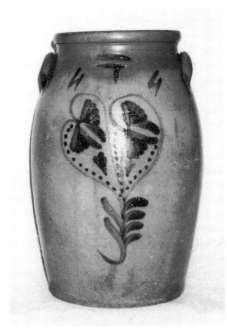

Rare signed Milwaukee, Wisconsin, four-gallon churn. $700–$900

Stenciled blue advertising jug, one gallon. $150–$200

Evan R. Jones, Pittston, Pennsylvania, 1½-gallon bale-handled batter pail, large brushed flower design. $700 *and up*

"Lyons," New York, two-gallon jug. $250–$300

Unsigned approximately two-gallon cake crock with matching lid. $400–$500

J.A. and C.W. Underwood, Ft. Edward, New York, two-gallon crock with large bird. $500–$600

E. and L.P. Norton, Bennington, Vermont, four-gallon crock. $500–$600

White's, Utica, two-gallon jug with rare compote of flowers decoration. $900–$1100

J.E. Norton, Bennington, Vermont, three-gallon jug with large and elaborate floral design. $1500 and up

F.B. Norton and Sons, Worcester, Massachusetts, uncommon 1½-gallon crock with blue dove decoration. $700–$900

One- and two-gallon jugs with uncommon "P. Mugler, Buffalo, N.Y." mark and blue brush decoration. $450–$550

Olean, New York, half-gallon batter pail, bale handle, undecorated. $150–$250; unsigned half-gallon Albany slip brown jug with incised store advertising, $50–$100.

John Burber, Rochester, New York, two-gallon crock, daisy decoration. $400–$500

Unsigned jug with "2 quarts" in blue script, New York state origin, $250–$350; "Lyons" one-gallon jug with simple plume design, $150–$200.

Riedinger and Caire, New York, four-gallon crock, long-tailed bird on a stump. $750–$950

J. Fisher, Lyons, New York, five-gallon crock with a blurred flower design. **$350–$450**; unsigned two-gallon crock with store advertising in blue script, **$150–$250**.

Unsigned three-gallon crock, **$275–$375**; six-quart bird crock, **$275–$375**.

Geddes, New York, four-gallon crock, large bird decoration, **$700–$800**; Brady and Ryan, Ellenville, New York, two-gallon bird on a stump, **$700–$800**.

"Lyons," New York, one-gallon jug, **$150–$200**; unsigned one-gallon ovoid jug, **$125–$175**.

N. Clark and Co., Athens, New York, ovoid crock dated "1868" in blue. **$650–$750**

J. and E. Norton, Bennington, Vermont, five-gallon crock with elaborate standing deer decoration. **$6000 an up**

J. and E. Norton, Bennington, Vermont, two-gallon jar **$700–$800;** *Cowden and Wilcox, Harrisburg, Pennsylvania, one-gallon cream pot,* **$225–$325.**

New York Stoneware, Ft. Edward, New York, one-gallon jug with large bird, **$500–$600;** *Ft. Edward Pottery Co., one-gallon bird jug,* **$400–$500.**

Unsigned three-gallon jug, New York state origin, **$300–$400;** *unsigned three-gallon bird crock with impressed store advertising,* **$350–$450.**

"Lyons," one-gallon lidded preserve jar, **$300–$400;** *"Lyons," one-gallon lidded preserve jar,* **$300–$400.**

John Burger, Rochester, New York, three-gallon churn with wreath design, **$400–$500;** *J. and C.W. Underwood, Ft. Edward, New York, large six-gallon bulbous churn,* **$400–$500.**

Ft. Edward Pottery, five-gallon crock with elaborate and rare double bird and plumes decoration. **$5000 and up**

Unsigned crock with "1871" in blue, with cover, Ohio origin, $350–$400; Hubbel and Cheboro, Geddes, New York, two-gallon jug, glaze worn off in spots, $100–$150.

T. Harrington, Lyons, New York, three-gallon crock with some grease staining. $450–$550

T. Harrington, Lyons, New York, six-gallon churn with the eagerly sought-after "starface" decoration on a churn. $7000 and up

J. and E. Norton, Bennington, Vermont, crock with rare dark blue reclining deer decoration. $3700 and up

John Burger, Rochester, New York, uncommon marked pouring pitcher. $800 and up

S. Hart, Fulton, New York, two-gallon jug with crossed love birds. $800–$950; unsigned cake crock with matching decorated lid. $650–$800

Burger and Lang, Rochester, New York, three-gallon crock with wreath design. $275–$375

Riedinger and Caire, Poughkeepsie, New York, two-gallon table churn with the centennial date "1876" in blue. $700–$900

J. Burger Jr., Rochester, New York, five-gallon crock with grapes, $400–$500; J. Burger Jr., Rochester, New York, three-gallon floral decorated crock, $350–$450.

Elaborately decorated five-gallon crock with spotted bird. $600 and up

133

6 *Textiles*

Individuals interested in hooked rugs, samplers, quilts, or coverlets have a unique advantage over other Americana collectors. In a throwaway society each generation tends to dispose of the household furnishings of its predecessors. Illinois and Ohio farm wives in the late nineteenth century were more than willing to trade handcrafted pine cupboards and tables for golden oak from the catalog stores in Chicago, Grand Rapids, and New York. When a decision was to be made about what happened to great-grandmother's sampler from 1824, Aunt Lydia's coverlet from Pennsylvania, or Cousin Edna's quilts, it usually resulted in a family debate about ownership.

As a society we usually revere the handcrafted items of the past that we can determine were made by our relatives. Uncle Ralph's bowling trophy or the 8′ coatrack with the broken mirror goes out the door much more quickly than a quilt, coverlet, or sampler that is functional or can be displayed in our homes. These items provide a link to our own past.

Quilts, coverlets, rugs, and samplers were cared for and kept after almost everything else was thrown out, given away, or relegated to the basement or barn. A collector cannot expect to find a blue pine cupboard at a closing-out farm auction in Idaho or West Virginia, but it is certainly within the realm of possibility that a century-old quilt will be pulled from a camelback trunk and offered for sale.

Quilt Chronology

1793   The textile industry in the United States was given a huge boost with the development of Eli Whitney's cotton gin that separated cotton seed from blossoms. This made cotton fabrics much less expensive to produce and more readily available to consumers.

1840s   Treadle, or foot-powered, sewing machines were being manufactured and utilized in some homes.

1850   Dry goods stores in most towns sold inexpensive cotton fabrics printed in a wide variety of designs at affordable prices.

1860s   The home sewing machine was commonly found across America. It is interesting to note that the Amish quilt makers were able to use treadle sewing machines because they were powered by foot movement.

1930s   Cotton thread was gradually replaced in most dry goods shops and department stores by a variety of synthetic threads.

Notes on Collecting Quilts

The earliest quilts were almost square in form. As beds became longer, quilts were made to be rectangular.

Since the 1930s, most quilt makers have used synthetic thread rather than the cotton variety. Cotton thread is difficult to find today.

One key to the quality of workmanship of a quilt is the number of stitches per inch. An old quilt should have a minimum of 12 stitches per inch. A quilt with 15 to 20 stitches per inch usually demonstrates exceptional workmanship.

Reproduction quilts are made for profit. Shortcuts are taken to save labor time and increase profitability. Most 50 to 75 year old quilts were created as gifts for loved ones and a great deal of care went into their production.

It is not uncommon for early full-size quilts that have been in use for many years to be cut down and have the bindings redone for use as crib quilts. Keep in mind that cribs are a twentieth-century innovation. In the nineteenth century, cradles or trundle beds were used for children. Typical "crib" quilts

Cotton "Baskets" quilt, brown-and-beige patched on white; sold at auction for $500 at Sotheby Parke-Bernet November 17–19, 1977.

Applique "Tulip" quilt, Pennsylvania German, c. 1840.

are found in sizes ranging from 22″ × 22″ to 44″ × 42″.

In evaluating a quilt, there are several primary considerations, including: usefulness, workmanship, originality of design, and condition, as well as colors and visual appeal. In nineteenth-century America applique quilts were used for show, or "best," and pieced quilts were in daily use.

When a quilt is folded for short-term or long-term storage, it should be folded a different way each time. Some experts recommend rolling, rather than folding, quilts. Store in pillowcases or other fabric—*never* in plastic—for protection.

Applique "House" quilt, c. 1875, 82″ × 79″.

Pieced quilt, red, white and blue, with white stars, stitched vine border, backing is blue and white homespun. Sold at Garth's Auctions, Delaware, Ohio, in 1977, for $160.

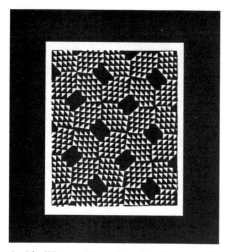

Amish "Ocean Waves" quilt, blue, purple, pink, grey, navy, green and white. Sold for $500 at Sotheby Parke-Bernet November 17–19, 1977.

The market for most quilts has softened in recent years. Dealers indicate that spectacular examples still bring big dollars, but more common quilts have regressed in value in many instances. Quilts with the quality of the five illustrated here continue to increase in value because they are rare and in demand from dealers and collectors. We are often asked about price trends for country antiques. Even in difficult economic times, items of quality at least hold their worth, and most continue to escalate in value.

Terms you'll need to understand include: *applique* (patches sewn on a base, sewing a piece cut from one piece of fabric directly onto a ground fabric, sometimes described as laid-on) and *pieced* (made by sewing straight-edged pieces of fabric together to form a top).

Examples of Collectible Textiles

The rugs, quilts, samplers, and coverlets shown here were recently sold at auction by Garth's Auctions of Delaware, Ohio.

Hooked yarn rug, two lions in a jungle with intricate design in rich colors, corner dated "1922." $700

Hooked rag rug, colorful folk art scene of Conestoga wagon with six horses, minor edge damage, mid-twentieth century, 25" × 48". **$265**

Hooked rag and yarn rug, finely detailed winter scene with many colors, grey border, turned edge of burlap selvage signed and titled "Home in the Wilderness," 23½" × 34½". **$295**

Pieced quilt, stylized geometric basket design in brown, teal blue, white, and red and green prints, some wear, stains, slight fading, 67" × 80". **$425**

Hooked rag and yarn rug, intricately detailed scene of seaside house and garden with harbor and lighthouse, 33" × 50". **$430**

Hooked rag rug, red barn, cow, two pigs, and tree, 25" × 34½". **$450**

139

Applique quilt, four large floral medallions in red, green, orange, and beige on a white ground, colors somewhat faded, 69" × 86". **$450**

Double weave two-piece coverlet, navy blue and natural, white snowflake and pine tree pattern, some wear, one seam resewn, fringe incomplete, and some patches, 65" × 85". $160.

Hooked rag and yarn rug, flowers and leaves in shades of red, blue, and green, good color, some minor wear, 36" × 52". $70

Contemporary Amish or Mennonite pieced crib quilt, star pattern, magenta on blue with black grid, 31" × 31", $45; contemporary Amish or Mennonite pieced crib quilt, red and blue nine-patch on a black ground, 22½" × 29", $185.

Applique quilt, stylized floral design in light green, red, and pale yellow, some overall wear and stains, red binding accent is worn and fabric is a bit fragile, 74" × 79". $600

Applique quilt, stylized floral medallions in red, pink, and brown calico on an off-white ground, binding is worn, 84" × 84". **$550**

Hooked rag rug, folk landscape in bright colors, minor wear and damage, 30" × 46". **$225**

Pieced quilt, basket design in calico in two shades of pink, green, and light bluish white with small red flower design, brown and white homespun back, 78" × 81". **$450**

*Jacquard two-piece single weave coverlet, "Knox County, Ohio 1845," 72″ × 88″, **$250;** jacquard two-piece double weave coverlet, "1836 Groton, N. York," 80″ × 86″, **$250;** jacquard two-piece single weave coverlet, "Johnsville, Morrow County, Ohio, 1851, wove by Josiah Cover," 76″ × 80″, **$275**.*

*Jacquard two-piece double weave coverlet, four rose medallions and stars with corners labeled "Mary Ann Dycart 1841," navy blue and natural white, 80″ × 88″. **$400***

145

Applique quilt, stylized floral design in green calico, solid red and yellow, applique letters "W" and "E" in corner, worn, and some fabrics are frayed, 78" × 78". **$350**

Pieced quilt, stylized tulip design in brown, green, and white solids, 72" × 86". $400

Applique crib quilt, stylized tulip medallion in solid goldenrod, purple, and greyish brown calico on a red ground, 34" × 34". **$285**

Pieced quilt, blue and white Irish chain, hand-sewn in large stitches, stains, wear, and minor repair, 69" × 83". **$115**

Pieced and knotted doll-size comforter, machine sewn, probably from a larger quilt, 15 ¾″ × 20½″, **$45;** *candlestand, refinished birch base and mismatched mahogany top, delicate spider legs, turned column and dish top, repairs to base where legs join, and repaired cracks in one-board top,* **$125.**

Single weave two piece coverlet, tan and natural white optical pattern with woven fringe on three sides, 85" × 95", $275; rope bed, refinished poplar, high turned feet and urn-like finials, replaced side rails, $100.

Pieced quilt, four-patch in blue, white, and beige calico, very worn, 67" × 76", $85; ladderback armchair rocker, old mellow refinishing, replaced woven seat, 44½" high, $250.

Appliqued wall hanging, nine panels with stylized flowers and berries on an off-white cotton gauze, machine-sewn red binding has some holes, 56" × 57", $330; ovoid stoneware jar, applied handles and impressed "3," stylized floral design in cobalt, rim chip, and old glued hole in side. Interior has worn white paint. $71.50

152

Pieced quilt, tumbling block in multicolored prints that are predominately maroon, black, white, blue, and red and white stripe, 65" × 72", **$400;** *country dry sink, poplar with several layers of old worn green paint,* **$575.**

Applique quilt, stylized floral design with tulips and oak leaves in two shades of solid green and red, 80" × 80". **$440**

Sampler, silk on dark linen homespun, rows of alphabets and geometric designs with stylized animals, trees, flowers, and "Ann Thomas Her work in the 13th year of her Age 1823," 18¼" × 11" (upper left), **$990;** *sampler, silk on homespun, alphabets, numerals, crows, trees, birds and "Mary Steel in the 6th year of her age 1793," framed, 13½" × 9½" (bottom right),* **$1100.**

Applique quilt, stylized floral medallions in red and green calico on a white ground, scalloped edges, twentieth century, 84" × 101". **$440**

Jacquard two-piece single weave coverlet, blue and natural white, bird and double-headed eagle borders with four rose medallions and corner labeled "Gabriel Rausher 1847," 66" × 86", **$495**; decorated blanket chest, poplar with original reddish brown flame graining, turned feet, dovetailed case and base and lid edge moldings, till removed, **$990**.

Mennonite pieced crib quilt, single star in multicolored solids on a white ground, 36" × 36", **$300**; Eastern woodlands Indian woven splint basket with lid, blue bands and curliques, some damage, 16" diameter × 13" high, **$205**.

Semicircular hooked rag rug, floral design in brown, orange, faded green, pink, and white on a dark blue and purple ground 25" × 34", **$70**; ovoid stoneware jug, grey salt glaze amber highlights, brown brushed tulip, and "2", 13¼" high, **$185**.

Jacquard one-piece single weave coverlet, blue and natural white, star center and eagle corners, wear and damage, 70" × 82". **$330**

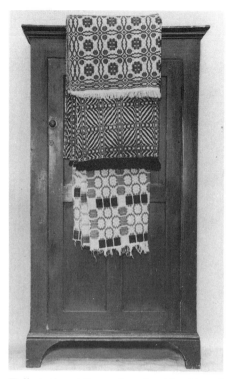

Jacquard two-piece double weave coverlet, navy blue and natural white with floral designs, pots of flowers in border, and edges labeled "United We Stand Divided We Fall, 1841," 76" × 88". **$357.50**

Tall poplar jelly cupboard with old red, bracket feet, four-panel door, solid ends, and molded cornice, 72" high, **$1540;** *three overshot coverlets, worn condition,* **$49.50– $82.50** *each.*

Applique quilt, twelve stylized floral medallions in red, yellow, and green calico with vining border in green calico, stains, 76" × 98". **$495**

Pieced quilt, pine tree pattern in green calico on a white ground, 92" × 110". $715

Jacquard one-piece single weave, floral medallion with women in spandrels, red and white, worn, fringe damage, and one corner is soiled, 82″ × 82″. **$165**

Applique quilt, four large scalloped edge flowers and border fans in beige, goldenrod, and red; stains and some fading, 84″ × 84″. **$660**

Pieced quilt, three dimensional tumbling blocks pattern in black and dark solid colors, some wear, stains, and small holes, 70" × 78". **$192.50**

Applique quilt, stylized floral medallions in teal green, red, and goldenrod, beautifully quilted with quilted designs having an almost trapunto appearance, stains, 67" × 76". **$440**

Pieced quilt, stars and sawtooth border, in green calico and yellow green and brown, pronounced diagonal bands of feather-quilted trapunto work, color fading, stains, and wear, 70" × 82". **$275**

Pieced quilt, star design, red calicos, solid greens, and white with red and goldenrod border stripes, with multi-color print pinwheel designs and navy blue calico in nine patch corners, 92" × 93", overall wear and some fading. **$275**

Jacquard one-piece single weave, central floral medallion with capital buildings in border, red, green, and natural, overall and edge wear, wool damaged in places, 77" × 81". **$165**

Pieced and applique quilt, nine large stars in green red and pink calico with green calico vining border, excellent quilting, made near Crittendon, Kentucky, stains and some color fading, 90" × 96". **$1705**

162

Pieced album or friendship quilt, multi-colored calico on white in a pink calico grid, center crosses each have a printed name, binding replaced and some localized stains and fading, 78" × 87". **$220**

Pieced quilt, log cabin medallion in brightly colored prints and solids, some wear, 70″ × 71″.
$275

Pieced crazy quilt, colorful satin, sateen and velvet with embroidery, worn, and some fabrics are frayed, 56" × 58". **$165;** *paint-decorated blanket chest, poplar with original yellow paint and brown combed graining, dovetailed case and dovetailed bracket feet with scrolled design on all four sides, large till with lid,* **$687.50**.

Pieced quilt, seventy-two stylized flowers in red and teal blue print, and red three-part border designs, beautifully quilted, stains, 95" × 100". $660

Hooked rag rug, dog in black, grey, and brown on a varied beige striped ground, wear and some edge damage, 21" × 38", **$357.50;** *decorated youth size Windsor rocker, old yellowed white repaint with black and gold striping and foliage scrolls, 28½" high,* **$247.50.**

Jacquard two-piece single weave coverlet, "Made by J. Wirick in St. Paris, Champaign Co., Ohio 1855 for Elizabeth Stuart," 68" × 76", **$440;** *country Sheraton blanket chest, figured walnut with old mellow finish, Kentucky or Tennessee origin,* **$605.**

Applique quilt, four large oak-leaf medallions in red and ecru, 77″ × 83″, **$275;** *southern cupboard, yellow pine with old mellow refinishing,* **$3190**.

Pieced quilt, Irish chain with flying geese border in red and white, worn and stained, and red has holes and fading, 78" × 79", **$170.50;** *country dry sink, refinished poplar, damage to base, and feet replaced,* **$440**.

Applique quilt, bold overall floral design in green, red, yellow, maroon, and pink calico, and solid red, stains, 86" × 102". **$2970**

Sampler, silk on linen homespun, finely detailed with a variety of stitches in old soft colors, vining floral border, "Elizabeth Peach, aged Eleven years," 21½" high × 20" wide (upper left), **$990;** *sampler, silk on linen homespun, alphabets, flowers, trees, verse, "Sarah Bower age 14, 1835," bird's-eye maple frame (lower left),* **$385.**

*Sampler, silk on homespun linen, vining strawberry border, alphabets, two dogs, and "Eliza Hopkins." Good color, unframed, 19" high × 13" wide, (upper left), **$385**; sampler, silk and wool on homespun linen. "Eliza Jane Riffels work, September 10th, 1827, Aged 12 years," 21" high × 16½" wide, (bottom right), **$550**.*

7 *Auctions, Shops, and Markets*

Copake Country Auctions

Michael Fallon is an auctioneer and appraiser who conducts cataloged Americana auction sales of formal and country furniture, Shaker items, quilts, coverlets, hooked rugs, samplers, and folk art. He is a member of the National Association of Certified Auctioneers, National Auctioneers' Association, New England Appraisers' Association, and the International Society of Appraisers.

The items that follow have been sold recently at Copake Country Auctions. Mr. Fallon may be contacted at:

Copake Country Auctions
Box H
Copake, NY 12516
Telephone: (518) 329-1142

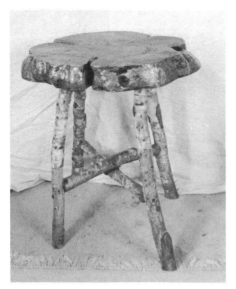

Tiger maple (top) and birch Adirondack table. **$425**

Miniature tramp art commode. **$660**

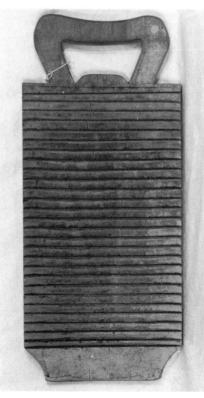

Primitive washboard. **$450**

Eighteenth-century wrought-iron candleholder. **$825**

176

Nineteenth-century Windsor settee. **$800**

Rhode Island Windsor chair, **$450**; *jug with bird decoration,* **$175**; *batter jug with floral decoration,* **$175**; *tavern table,* **$675**.

Early twentieth-century baseball picture. **$275**

Basket of tulips quilt. **$250**

Cast-iron Shaker stove. **$450**

Early pine chimney cupboard. **$1200**

Quebec, Canada, nineteenth-century armoire, pine. **$770**

Snowflake quilt. **$550**

Pembroke table, New York City, c. 1810. **$2000**

Canadian Fleur-de-Lis quilt, c. 1930. **$275**

179

Pennsylvania applique quilt. $575

Nineteenth-century Pennsylvania Dutch cupboard. **$1500**

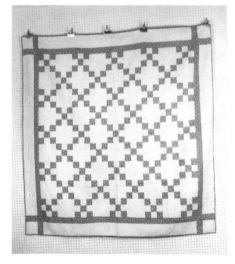

Nine-patch quilt. $330

Lancaster Antique Market

The 10,000 square-foot Lancaster Antique Market in Lancaster, Kentucky, was recently described by the New York Times as being "the best small-town antiques center in Kentucky."

Travel and Leisure magazine said "Surprisingly, the antiquing here surpasses any other Bluegrass town."

Rose Holtzclaw and Ellen Tatem, owners of the market, produce a monthly video of merchandise that they have recently purchased for resale. The 30 to 40 minute narrated videotape may be purchased for a fee of $10. Antiques are shipped daily by United Parcel Service and freight.

Available for visitors to the Market

is a bed and breakfast located in an 1815 Federal-style house situated in a rural setting on fifteen acres.

The address of the Market is:

Lancaster Antique Market
102 Hamilton Ave.
P.O. Box 553
Lancaster, KY 40444
Telephone: (606) 792-4536

Questions and Answers

Rose Holtzclaw and Ellen Tatem, the owners of the country-oriented Lancaster Antique Market in Lancaster, Kentucky, answered some questions for us.

Q. What is the current market for refinished country furniture?

A. Customers who buy furniture manufactured from 1900 on prefer refinished furniture.

Q. What is the market for painted furniture?

A. Good, one of a kind, country pieces still sell better for us in old paint or original finish.

Q. How about Shaker?

A. The market here has been good for the production rocking chairs made by the Shakers. Our customers feel more comfortable with pieces that they can readily recognize as Shaker.

Q. In the past year has interest grown in any one particular category of Americana?

A. The past year has been good for folk art. The pieces that are made well, and rare pieces, sell much better than the common ones.

Q. Has interest diminished in any category?

A. Homespun fabrics and linens have not sold as well recently as in the past. Quilts are still selling well here.

Q. In the early 1990s watering cans went from a single digit in price to almost three digits in many parts of the United States. Are there any country collectibles that are specifically hot right now?

A. Birdhouses are selling great for us. We like the older ones but we can sell most any one we find regardless of age.

Q. In your antiques market how do you maintain or monitor the quality of the merchandise the dealers offer for sale?

A. We try to keep our dealers aware of what merchandise is selling well. The better things sell first. This helps some in maintaining quality.

Q. Among the various categories of Americana (furniture, textiles, pottery, advertising, kitchen and hearth antiques) is there an area that you feel that is currently underpriced?

A. We believe that good American furniture is currently underpriced. Most smalls seem overpriced to us.

Kentucky basket with "kicked-up" bottom and a 9" opening. **$125**

A folksy green table made from a sassafras root. **$95**

Birdhouse with red roof and chimney. **$45**

Octagon-shaped wooden box with hinged lid and decorative paint. **$395**

Decorative gate used as a wall hanging. **$245**

Nine-foot table in mustard paint with decorated leg supports. **$850**

Five-inch Shaker fingered box, signed and dated. $595}

Shaker-style bucket in painted finish with coffin-shaped brace used to support wire handle. $175

Shaker rocker #1. $1200

Tramp art mirror in red, gold, and black paint. $265

Wooden box with tray decorated in green paint. $145

Pine tree quilt in green and white. **$595**

Small tin candle lantern, 8" high. **$85**

Red-and-white quilt in mint condition. **$595**

Tin candle lantern with star cutouts. **$195**

Hickory splint baby basket, 1890, 36" in length. **$175**

"Welcome" hooked rug, 25" × 36", **$265**.

Wooden duck decoy, brown, beige, and black. **$295**

Red-and-white quilt with small sawtooth border. **$495**

Painted sled with optional rolling wheels. **$145**

Detail of a pantry box, painted blue, with "drop" handle. Shaker-type diamond brackets on side, 34" diameter, **$300–$375**

Golden Drop Plums bucket with "drop handle," painted finish and paper label, late nineteenth century. **$325–$375**

Apple butter bucket, paper label, late nineteenth century, painted gray. **$300–$375**

186

Rare sugar bucket with "button-hole" hoops, nineteenth century. **$400–$475**

Late nineteenth-century sugar bucket, factory-made, painted blue, "drop handle," 6" diameter top. **$300–$335**

Shaker, "Harvard" butter box, 14" diameter, painted yellow, button-hole hoops. **$425–$475**

Twentieth-century bucket, stapled fingers, painted grey, 4" diameter (top), c. 1920s–1930s. **$300–$350**

Shaker oval box, 15", original stained finish. **$750–$1000**

Shaker oval box, maple and pine, painted blue, copper nails, 7" box. **$1000–$1500**

One-half pound butter mold, factory made, maple, c. early 1900s, with rare cow decoration. **$300–$350**

Maple mortar and pestle, painted green, late nineteenth century. **$300–$325**

Turned wooden pestle, maple. **$40–$50**

Turned wooden bowl, 11" diameter, maple, painted finish, c. late nineteenth century. **$175–$200**

American eagle butter print, 4" diameter. $400–$450

One-half basket, white oak. $140–$160

Late nineteenth-century tin strainer. $25–$30

Buttocks basket with twisted splint handle, found in New York. $250–$300

Wooden grocer's scoop made of a single piece of maple, early 1900s. $300–$350

Three turned wooden bowls, nineteenth-century, maple, original painted finish, 4" to 8" diameters. $135–$200 each

Storage basket, carved handles, "kicked-in" bottom, 11" diameter. **$225–$250**

Oak runners or braces on the bottom of the wash basket.

Splint wash basket, early twentieth century. **$300–$350**

Pennsylvania rye straw basket. **$95–$115**

Splint utility basket, carved handle, double wrapped rim, 10" diameter. **$200–$225**

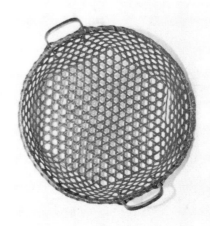

"Cheese-weave" drying basket, New England, nineteenth century. **$300–$350**

190

Utility or storage basket, carved handles, double-wrapped rim. **$225–$250**

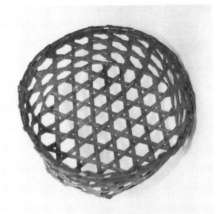

Cheese basket, found in New York state, 26″ diameter. **$650–$900**

Cast-iron coffee grinder, c. late nineteenth century, original condition. **$675–$800**

Folk art birdhouse, original painted decoration, c. early 1900s. **$175–$200**

Six-gallon midwestern water cooler, c. early 1900s, double handles. **$200–$285**

Feather Christmas tree, turned base, original condition, c. 1920, 18" tall, made in Germany. **$275–$350**

Feather Christmas tree, German origin, 16" tall, original condition. **$250–$275**

Leaf butter print, maple, twentieth century. **$75–$85**

Rare cow butter print with detail, c. late nineteenth century. **$350–$450**

Deeply carved red rose butter print, maple.
$300–$350

Pineapple butter print, nineteenth century.
$250–$300

Detailed butter print, nineteenth century.
$250–$300

Leaves and acorns butter print. **$200–$250**

*Child's homemade rocking horse, c. early
twentieth century, original painted finish.*
$350–$400

*Collection of factory-made butter molds, early
twentieth century, maple, simple geometric
designs or leaves.* **$85–$100** *each*

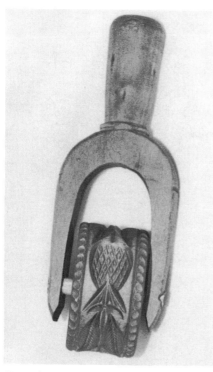

Tin country store scoop, hanging hook, c. early 1900s. **$20–$25**

"Lollipop" style butter print, possibly European in origin, nineteenth century. **$175–$225**

Rare butter print, nineteenth century. **$450–$500**

Lorraine's Country Sampler Collection

Lorraine's Country Sampler Collection specializes in authentic early Americana, painted furniture, and smalls. The shop also carries an extensive collection of nineteenth-century decorated stoneware. Lorraine's Country Sampler Collection may be contacted by telephone at (206) 334-2323. The business is located in Snohomish, Washington, and is open by appointment.

Two-gallon Pennsylvania cake crock with lid, strong cobalt decoration. **$600–$700**

194

Edmonds and Co. crock, speckled bird with lots of leaves. $1500

Edmonds and Co., two-gallon cream pot with a reclining and spotted deer. $3500 plus

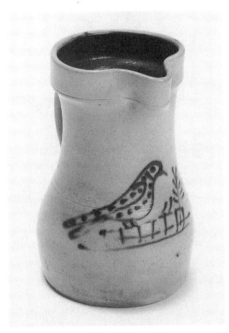

Edmonds and Co. bird with fence milk pitcher, uncommon. $1900

Two-gallon J. & E. Norton, Bennington, Vermont jug, bird on a stump, rare, heavy cobalt. $1400

One-and-one-half gallon Bennington, Vermont crock. **$750** *plus*

Edmonds and Co. four-gallon bird crock. **$550–$650**

One-gallon jug, J. & E. Norton, Bennington, Vermont bird on a stump. **$1200–$1500**

Four-gallon jug with long-tailed bird, probably from New York Stoneware Co., Ft. Edward, New York. **$650**

Three-gallon jug, F. E. Norton and Co., Worcester, Massachusetts, $700–$800

One-gallon jug, J. Norton Co. Bennington, Vermont $600–$700

Two-gallon jar with bird, signed W. Roberts, Binghamton, New York. $600–$700

E. and L.P. Norton, Bennington, Vermont jar. $700–$800

197

One-gallon W. Roberts jar with folky bird.
$800

Two-gallon crock with bird, T. Harrington,
Lyons, New York. $1000–$1100

Two-gallon jug, Whites, Utica, New York co-
balt bird. $750

One-gallon jug, with bird. New York Stone-
ware C., Ft. Edward, New York. $450–
$550

Four-quart unsigned batter jug, probably Whites, Utica, New York. **$1000–$1200**

Unsigned jar, one-gallon, with bird. **$500**

One-gallon jug with unusual cobalt bird, unsigned. **$500–$600**

Unsigned two-gallon bird jug. **$550–$650**

One-gallon West Troy, New York, whiskey jug with primitive decoration, handle and cork. $500–$600

Five-gallon butter churn, Adam Caire. $600–$750

One-gallon crock with running bird, Whites, Utica, New York. $550–$650

One-gallon jar with bird, unsigned. $700

200

One-half-gallon incised Pennsylvania milk pitcher. **$950**

Two-gallon butter churn with deep cobalt decoration, Lyons, New York. **$650–$750**

One-gallon butter crock with lid. **$450–$550**

One-half gallon jug with tulips, unsigned. **$350**

Small butter crock. $300–$350

Small half-gallon milk pitcher. $500–$600

Six-inch jar, impressed "½" on opposite side.
$300–$400

*One-half gallon jug, slip-trailed decoration,
unsigned.* $300–$400

*Probable butter crock or jar, unusual size,
strong blue decoration.* $650

Small crock with lid. $300–$350

Cream pot with strong blue, Pen Yan, New York. $375

One-half gallon ovoid jug, early nineteenth century. $550–$650

Small jar, double flowers, strong blue decoration. $285

Cream pot, Williamsport, Pennsylvania.
$475–$525

Store jar, W.R. Beall & Co., Cumberland, Maryland. **$650** *plus*

W. Moyer jar with lid, brushed cobalt design.
$300 *plus*

Three-gallon jar, Pennsylvania origin. **$500** *plus*

Four-quart batter jug, New York state. **$500** plus

Preserve jar, 6½" tall, **$285**; stoneware cup, 4" tall, **$225**.

Oyster basket from Maine, wonderful patina, excellent condition. **$325** plus

One-gallon Burlington, Vermont, jug with heavy cobalt decoration. **$850–$950**

Potato stamp basket. **$95**

Early child's high chair with great blue paint.
$1000 *plus*

Large blue churn, complete original condition. **$695** *plus*

Child's backpack basket. **$185** *plus*

Small blue painted splint basket. **$250** *plus*

Rye straw basket from Pennsylvania. **$395** *plus*

Splint basket with carved handles and wrapped rim. **$265** *plus*

Early cupboard in original red paint over grey. **$4000** *plus*

Pantry cupboard in blue paint from Maine. **$3000**

Six-tube candlemold, **$350** *up; tin candle holder,* **$195** *plus; four-tube candle mold, probably for church candles,* **$595**; *tin fuel filler with two spouts,* **$195**; *rush light,* **$425** *plus.*

Collection of items in original blue paint.

Pewter and Wood

A shop called Pewter and Wood is noted for its variety of quality eighteenth- and nineteenth-century Americana. Barbara Boardman Johnson, the shop's owner, has been collecting antiques for more than twenty-five years. Having grown up in Connecticut and lived in Vermont, she returns to the East and Midwest several times a year.

Pewter and Wood contains a selection of unusual and hard-to-find "smalls" and furniture in original paint, as well as pine, cherry, and walnut. Cupboards abound with majolica, flow blue, quilts, primitives, and decorated stoneware. Children's items, wooden blocks, folk art, and textiles are nestled in the room settings. Fresh dried herbs and flowers add a touch of New England to the desert shop.

Pewter and Wood is located in Scottsdale, Arizona. Shop hours are 10 a.m. to 5 p.m. Monday through Saturday, and by appointment. Shipping is available, and collectors and dealers are welcome.

Pewter and Wood
10636 N. 71st Way, #14
Scottsdale, AZ 85254
Telephone: (602) 948-2060

Stack of footstools, New England and Pennsylvania, nineteenth century, original paint, mortised construction, **$125–$250** *each; cutlery tray in bittersweet paint,* **$275;** *straw-stuffed jointed bear, working growler,* **$225–$350;** *blue child's rocking chair, nineteenth century,* **$175–$195**.

Bail-handled pantry boxes, New England, late nineteenth century, **$400–$600;** *six-drawer spice box, square nails,* **$425–$485;** *Enterprise #3 double wheel coffee grinder, original paint, decoration, and drawer,* **$700–$750**.

House, c. 1920s–1930s, 16½" deep × 12" wide × 12" high, original condition. **$275–$350**

Small chest with graduated drawers, nineteenth century, original old red paint, square nails, **$850–$895;** *folk art doll, wooden head, painted face and cloth body,* **$300–$340.**

Mustard apothecary, New England, twelve dovetailed drawers, c. 1850s, 32" long × 10" high, **$1400–$1600;** *New England pantry boxes with drop handles, nineteenth century, original painted finish,* **$375–$695.**

Pantry boxes, nineteenth century, in original paint, $185–$395 each; cutlery tray, heart cutout handle, old blue paint, $270–$285; nineteenth-century mortar and pestle, 4" high, green paint, $260–$285; New England, late nineteenth-century black doll, $130–$150; twelve-drawer apothecary chest, c. 1850, original finish, $425–$475; red-painted six-board box, mid-nineteenth century, New England, $275–$350.

Straw-stuffed bear, and cart in original paint, wheels replaced, $365–$425; child's potty chair in original paint, with blue and white homespun upholstered seat, $475–$525; jointed bear, straw stuffed, glass eyes, c. 1900s, $450–$495.

Horse on swing frame, nineteenth century, hide-covered, leather reins and saddle replaced; frame has original red paint with original decoration, excellent condition. **$1000–$1200**

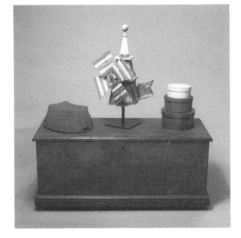

Folk art windmill whirlygig, original old red, white, and blue paint, New England, c. early 1900s, **$675–$700;** *stack of three pantry boxes, ½"–9½", red, white and blue,* **$1250–$1285** *stack; decorated six-board box, old red paint with smoke decoration, dovetailed, c. mid-nineteenth century,* **$695–$795.**

New England nineteenth-century gameboard, original paint, $695–$795; set of 26 embossed ABC blocks, 2" × 2" each, $275; New England nineteenth-century gameboard, original paint, square nailed, $695–$795.

Doll cupboard, southern pine, pegged construction, c. 1860s–1880s, $395–$495; German Santa, 13" tall, composition face, rabbit fur beard, orange cloth coat, $685–$885; doll quilt, New England, log cabin design, c. 1870s, $295–$350; buttermolds, nineteenth century, $95–$135.

Stack of firkins, New England, mustard, green, and red, $1300–$1400 stack; gameboard, doublesided, c. 1880s, red and black with mustard striping, $650–$695; "under the wagon seat" basket in original salmon paint, $350–$395.

Hanging pine corner cupboard, scalloped shelves, pegged and mortised door, c. 1850s–1870s, $800–$875; Sheraton-style pine washstand with pitcher and bowl, $495.

Maple rope bed, acorn finials, quilt rail, Missouri origin, c. 1860s, $700–$775; blue six-board box, dovetailed, Pennsylvania, signed and dated "1832," $495–$695.

215

Walnut stepback cupboard, two-piece, raised panel doors, original glass, dovetailed drawers, Missouri, c. 1860s–1870s. **$2500–$2900**

Corncob decorated painted apothecary, Pennsylvania, **$900–$975;** *Enterprise No. 7 coffee grinder with eagle and original paint and decoration,* **$900;** *blue butter-churn, New York state,* **$400–$475.**

Red canteen, staved construction, c. 1860s, signed "A. Slind," **$225;** *New York state gameboard, nineteenth century, red and black,* **$695;** *ship lantern, brass with green paint, original green glass, A. Tafts Bros., c. 1860;* **$250.**

Stack of green boxes, all in original paint, New England and New York state, c. 1840s–1870s. **$250–$700** each

Pine stepback cupboard, New Hampshire origin, 50" wide × 78½" high. **$2400–$2600**

Vermont open pewter cupboard in pine; rosehead nails, plate grooves, refinished, **$995;** collection of American and continental pewter, nineteenth century, **$50–$395** each.

217

Bowl of stone fruit, eighteen pieces, $650–$750; nineteenth-century game board, double-sided with two drawers, original paint, $800–$975.

Refinished table from a New England dry goods store, $1495; set of six Pennsylvania decorated chairs in original paint, $1900–$2200.

Collection of blue-and-white spongeware, $275–$350 each; group of butter stamps, early to mid-nineteenth century, Pennsylvania origins, $225–$495 each.

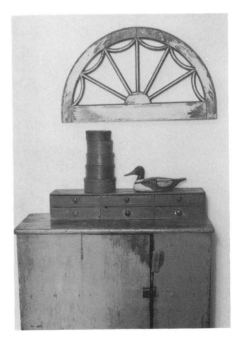

Architectural window from New England, late nineteenth century. $395

8 *Graniteware*

G raniteware was a popular item in American kitchens from the 1860s through the early 1930s. It was manufactured by putting a double- or triple-coated enamel surface over iron or steel base metals.

Collectors are interested in a wide range of graniteware utensils, including toiletry articles, pots, pans, spoons, buckets, sinks, stoves, butter churns, and dustpans. Advertising pieces that feature graniteware are also eagerly collected.

Graniteware Chronology

1830s	Manufactured in Europe.
1860s	Introduced with mixed success into the United States.
1870s–early 1890s	Graniteware was made with cast-iron handles.
1876	The Philadelphia Exposition featured several exhibitors of graniteware and new interest among homemakers was sparked.
early 1900s	Graniteware was made with wooden handles.
1914	World War I forced numerous European makers to produce military goods rather than graniteware. Austrian and German manufacturers of graniteware were especially affected by the war.
1930s	Production of aluminum household goods changed the buying patterns of American homemakers, and graniteware was no longer as popular; production significantly decreased.

Questions and Answers

Hennepin, Illinois, graniteware dealers Gary and Lorraine Boggio responded to our questions about the current state of the market for their specialty.

Q. If you were going to start a collection of graniteware today, what would you collect?

A. Unusual pieces of any color in very good condition. Condition is critical.

Q. In the past year has any one color or type of piece of graniteware had a significant increase in value?

A. Cobalt has increased by approximately 70 percent in value in the past two years.

Q. Are reproductions currently a major problem for graniteware collectors?

A. No. Because most collectors can distinguish between an old piece and a reproduction in several ways. The weight, color, and construction of an old piece of graniteware differ significantly from reproduction examples.

Q. Is there a book or price guide on graniteware that you would recommend for beginning collectors?

A. *Graniteware Collectors Book 1* and *Graniteware Collectors Book 2* for general information, and the *Collector's Encyclopedia of Graniteware* for pricing.

Q. From the standpoint of rarity, what is the ultimate piece of graniteware?

A. A very small or very unusual piece of graniteware in mint condition with a label or stamp in "old red."

Examples of Graniteware

The graniteware items shown are from the extensive collection and shop inventory of Gary and Lorraine Boggio of North Wind Antiques in Hennepin, Illinois.

The Boggios offer for sale one of the largest selections of pine furniture and graniteware in the Midwest. They have conducted an extensive mail business in graniteware for several years. The Boggios may be contacted:

North Wind Antiques
420 E. High St.
Hennepin, IL 61327
Telephone: (815) 925-7264

Gray oval dinner bucket. **$325–$375**

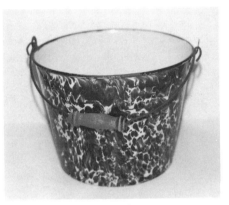

Chryosite bucket. **$250–$295**

Cobalt gooseneck teapot. **$450–$575**

Blue-and-white swirl dairy pan. **$150–$195**

Berry buckets, cobalt and blue-and-white swirl. **$250–$350** *each*

Syrup pitchers, white with cobalt and black trim. **$100–$120** *each*

Salt box, white with cobalt trim. **$225–$295**

Blue-and-white swirl Berlin-style pot. **$220–$300**

Tea kettle, white with cobalt trim. **$70–$95**

Columbian-ware bean pot. **$280–$350**

Gray milk pitchers. **$125–$180** *each*

Gray convex pitchers. **$160–$250** *each*

Cobalt canning funnel. **$130–$175**

Gray one-cup gooseneck coffee biggin. **$225–$295**

Gray frypan. **$75–$125**

Gray ladles. **$45–$65** *each*

Gray spoons. **$40–$75** *each*

Gray small teakettles. **$140–$195** *each*

Gray skimmers. **$45–$65** *each*

Gray scalloped mold. **$65–$95**

Blue-and-white swirl coffee cups. **$50–$65** *each*

Gray measures. **$140–$225** *each*

Gray side snipe ladle. **$140–$175**

Blue-and-white swirl coffeepot. **$200–$245**

Blue-and-white swirl gooseneck coffeepot. **$400–$495**

Cobalt coffeepot. **$240–$295**

Chryosite gooseneck teapots. **$350–$595** *each*

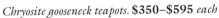

227

Gray dry measure. **$125–$160**

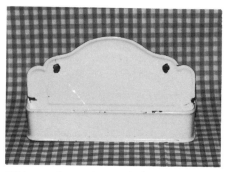

White comb case. **$250–$325**

Dry measure, white with cobalt trim. **$65–$95**

Gray round platter. **$60–$85**

Colander, white with cobalt trim. **$40–$58**

White percolator funnel. $95–$135

Sink strainer, white with black trim. $140–$165

Sink strainer, white with cobalt trim. $65–$85

Gray oval platter. $50–$75

Sugar bowl, white with cobalt trim. $160–$225; *creamer,* $140–$175.

229

9 *Country Store Antiques and Collectibles*

Late nineteenth- and early twentieth-century country stores were major social centers for small-town and rural America. The stores were usually located at a well-traveled crossroads or at a key spot in the middle of town. In the winter the cast-iron potbellied stove in the center of the store served as a beacon for locals looking for a checker game or an opportunity to discuss the latest gossip. Most of the stores also had a long front porch with well-used rocking chairs for lingering on a summer's day.

Among the diverse offerings of the typical country store were the following:

groceries	hardware	crockery
candy	toys	musical instruments
spices	clocks	tools
clothing	tinware	brooms and brushes
shoes and boots	coffee and tea	dishes
oysters	cider	baskets
locally grown fruits	medicines and miracle	string and rope
and vegetables	cures	sporting goods
cosmetics	meat	sewing supplies

Today's collectors are searching for every aspect of the country store from the screened front door to signs, containers, posters, and chopping blocks. If it was a part of the store, nailed to the store, or sold in the store, it is highly collectible.

Dating Country Store Items

The chronology that appears below is designed to assist collectors seeking to accurately date the country store antiques and collectibles that they may find. Careful study of the packaging of the item can be an invaluable tool in determining its age.

Packaging Chronology

1660s	Paper packages were used to wrap medicines.
1680	An advertisement in a London newspaper suggested that customers bring a box if they want to purchase tea.
Late 1600s	Wine bottles with specific tavern markings were in use in England and colonial America.
1750	Paper labels appeared on wine bottles.
1770s	Pottery jars were used for hair dressings, mustard, and medicines.
1800	Wooden boxes with paper labels were found in stores.
1840s	Metal "tin" foil was used to wrap individual chocolates and packages of tea and coffee.
After 1850	Matches and match boxes were in daily use in most homes. Liquid ink in glass or stoneware bottles was available in stationery stores. Butter and cigarettes were wrapped with paper packages.
Early 1850s	A patent was issued for a machine that makes paper bags.

Late 1850s	Cotton bags were used for packaging flour. Civil War demands for cotton caused a shortage of cotton and merchandisers turned to heavy paper. By 1870 paper bags could easily hold 50 to 75 pounds of flour.
Early 1870s	Paper bags are used by some stores for customers to carry home their purchases.
1873	Machines mass-produce paper bags; many more stores begin to use paper bags.
1880	Packages of cigarettes have stiffeners added to keep the contents from being smashed. The stiffeners evolve shortly into the first baseball cards.
1896	A company in Evansville, Indiana sells 500,000 bottle caps to Anheuser-Busch in St. Louis.
1898	The National Biscuit Company packages its products in moisture-proof boxes for use at home. The country store cracker barrel is put in the attic. Kraft cheese is available in family-size packages.
1900	Paper, pottery, metal, foil, glass, and wood are commonly used by food manufacturers in packaging their products.
1910	Aluminum foil is available to consumers.
1912	Cellophane is initially utilized in packaging.

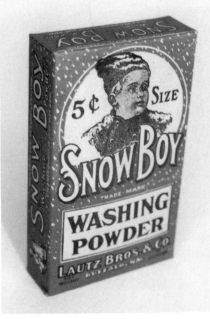

Rockford Farm Pure Sorghum container.
$35–$45

Snow Boy Washing Powder. **$25–30**

Fairy Soap box. **$25–$30**

Mi-Boy Coffee sack. **$6–$9**

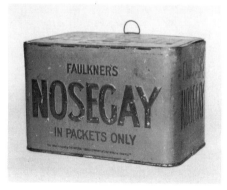

Faulkner's Nosegay counter container. **$85–$100**

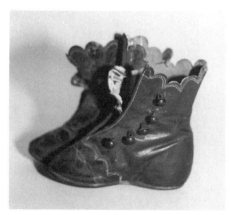

Child's leather button shoes. **$55–$60**

Wood framed tin sign for City Candy Kitchen and Restaurant. **$350–$450**

Wooden sidewalk sign for Eureka Steam Laundry, c. 1900. **$350–$400**

Barrel lid from Badger Brand Wisconsin Cranberries. **$150–$200**

Child's leather boots. **$25–$30**

Rare Gold Prize Coffee wall clock. $850–
$1000

Eveready Buckwheat Flour and Wheat Flour
box. $25–$30

Betty Zane Pop Corn box. $10–$15

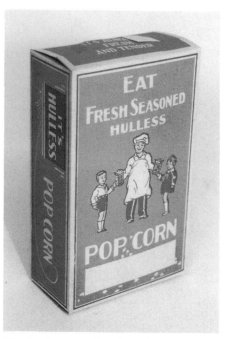

"Hulless" popcorn box. $10–$15

Tim's Cap box. **$30–$40**

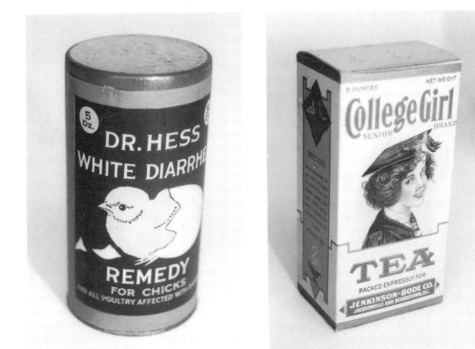

Dr. Hess White Diarrhea Remedy. **$12–$16**   *College Girl Tea container.* **$28–$32**

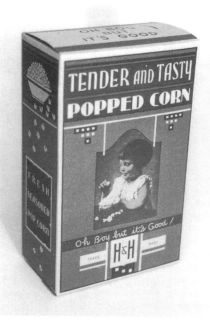

Box of Mother's Crushed Oats. $35–$45

Tender and Tasty Popped Corn box. $10–$20

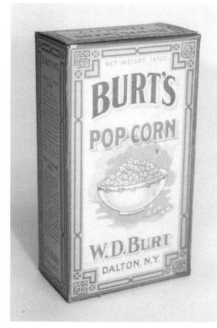

Burt's Pop Corn box. $10–$20

Butter-Kist popcorn box. $10–$20

Holstein Bell No. 3. $75–$85

Campbell Brand Coffee can. $30–$35

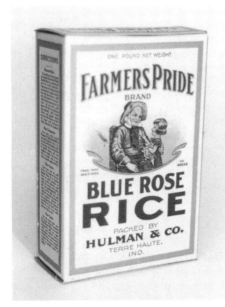

Blue Rose Rice box. $12–$16

Tomson's Red Seal Cleanser. $20–$30

Superior Pickles bottle with original paper labels. $75–$85

Mocha-Java Coffee can. $45–$55

Fresh Ground Chum Salmon cans. $8–$9 each

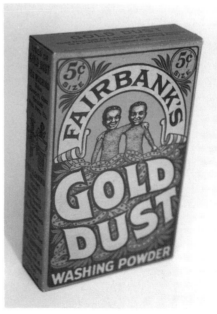

Fairbank's Gold Dust washing powder box. $40–$50

Late nineteenth-century Sugar Corn can.
$35–$45

LaCreole Hair Dressing bottle. **$35–$50**

Black Beauty Axle Grease can. **$50–$55**

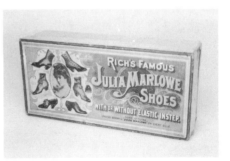

Rich's Famous Julia Marlowe Shoes box.
$15–$20

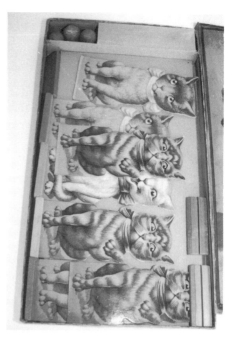

The Pussy Cat Ten Pins game. **$100–$115**

Royal Baking Powder price plaque. **$75–$85**

Thomson and Taylor Spice Co. coffee bin. **$300–$400**

1920s valentine. **$15–$20**

Box of stick cinnamon. **$8–$10**

Brown's French Dressing box. **$15–$18**

Walton Shoe box. **$30–$40**

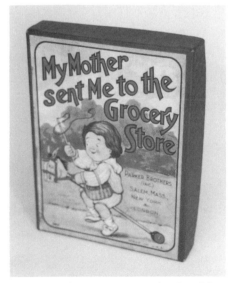

Parker Brothers game My Mother Sent Me to the Grocery Store. **$100–$120**

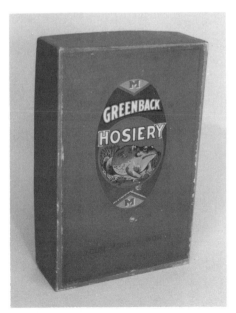

Greenback Hosiery box. **$25–$35**

Beautiebows display. $25–$35

Kentucky Cardinal Hosiery box. $20–$25

Fairbank's Gold Dust Washing Powder case.
$75–$100

Three-bar box of Woodbury's Facial Soap.
$20–$25

Gilliam's Blue Grass Candies box. $25–$35

Shoelace counter display. $75–$85

Tic-Toc dishwashing powder. **$8–$12**

Sharples Cream Separators sign. **$150–$200**

Pratts Poultry Regulator tonic. **$12–$15**

Bull Dog Liquid Spray Insecticide. **$18–$24**

Butler Brothers 1920 catalog. **$30–$40**

D. Crawford's New Store advertising stand-up c. 1905. **$130–$150**

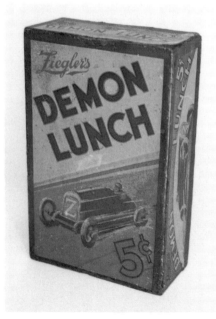

Demon Lunch 5¢ candy bar box. **$20–$25**

"Merry Christmas, Happy New Year" box, c. 1910. **$100–$125**

Rare Wedding Ring Coffee pail. **$125–$150**

Late nineteenth-century food can. **$35–$45**

Miniature Ezra Williams flower seed box, 8" long ;tx 4" wide. **$250–$325**

10 *Windmill Weights*

In 1853 Daniel Halladay of Ellington, Connecticut, invented a self-regulating windmill. As other windmill manufacturers entered the market, they needed some form of identifying logo to differentiate their windmills from those of a competitor.

Cast-iron regulator or counterbalance weights in the form of an animal, rooster, initial, or geometric shape eventually became the manner in which to advertise their windmills.

In the 1930s and 1940s, when electricity came to even the most remote rural areas, the windmill was no longer necessary to pump water and many of the windmills were taken apart or allowed to gradually fall down over the next several decades. World War II scrap metal drives also swallowed many derelict windmills.

In the late 1960s and early 1970s, antiques collectors first began to take notice of the cast-iron weights, and prices slowly began to rise. They now are rising at a much faster rate.

Terms

counterbalance weight: Usually heavy (30 to 140 pounds); served as a counterbalance to the windmill's flywheel.

regulator weight: Smaller than a counterbalance weight (8 to 15 pounds); used to maintain consistent revolution speed regardless of how fast the wind was blowing.

Elgin Wind Power and Pump Company "Hummer" rooster with a "short-stem," c. early 1900s–1930. The ball-shaped base could be separated and filled with scrap iron, metal, or rocks for additional weight. **$675–$875**

"Hummer" rooster. **$300–$500**

Elgin rooster. **$900–$1100**

250

Dempster "bob-tail" or short tail horse, c. early 1900s–1940. The bridle is a decoration addition. **$275–$375**

"Rainbow tail" with worn black paint. **$950–$1150**

Marked "Boss" bull that has lost its original ears and tail. **$385–$500**

Simpson Wind Mill and Machine Company, unmarked "Boss" or "Hanchett" bull. **$385–$500**

Althouse-Wheeler Company, Waupum, Wisconsin "W." **$550–$700**

Final Exam

Due to a constantly decreasing amount of mail, we are going to give you another opportunity for semi-immortality. If your score qualifies, you may be offered membership in the High Achiever's Club (HAC is made up of distinguished individuals who scored *at* or *above* the *ninth* percentile on previous editions of the Final Exam).

At a recent HAC meeting held in the parking lot of Sporty's Spot Lite Lounge on July 29, 1993, it was determined by a 5:2 vote of the six-person executive committee to award mimeographed certificates of merit, rather than a personal telephone call from the President of the HAC (the rumors about him are untrue and should *not* be repeated).

Directions

You may rest assured that the questions on this exam have been invalidated by an independent testing firm. Every expense has been spared to maintain the inaccuracy of the material that is covered by the questions that follow.

1. Open the test booklet to page 326 and disregard all previous directions.

2. Carefully read each question. Do *not* move your lips, as others may be watching. Keep in mind that "Loose lips give hints."

3. Use only recycled pencils and pens.

4. All food, beverages, and sharp objects should be removed from the room before taking the test.

Questions

Match the letter of the picture with the number of the phrase that best describes it:

1. made by the Shakers _____

2. "thrown" _____

3. a reproduction _____

4. "slip-trailed" _____

5. dates from about 1900 _____

6. "turned" _____

7. worth about $225 _____

8. Put a check (√) mark next to the statements below that are true.

A.

B.

C.

a. The watering can would be a "good buy" for $250.

b. This watering can dates from about 1890–1900.

c. It is made of oak and tin.

d. This jack-o-lantern is worth about $45–$55.

e. It dates from about 1900.

f. It is made of pressed paper.

9. Mary Earle Gould's book on colonial furniture is considered a classic.

   True ___ False ___

10. The *Antiques Review* was previously known as the *Maine Antiques Digest.*

    True ___ False ___

11. The legendary Brimfield show is located in New York state.

    True ___ False ___

12. Mahogany is a wood native to the American Southeast (North and South Carolina, Maryland).

    True ___ False ___

13. More handcrafted nineteenth-century American furniture was made of oak than of pine.

    True ___ False ___

14. Check (√) the statements below that are *true* about the basket.

___ It dates from the eighteenth century.

___ It is a cheese weave basket.

___ In blue paint it's worth at least $225.

255

___ It was factory made.

___ The handle was hand-carved.

___ The splint was cut by a machine rather than by hand.

___ The basket could be from as late as 1900.

15. Match the letter of the picture with the number of the statement that best describes it.

___ This piece is easily the most valuable.

___ This piece is the least valuable.

___ Decorated with a brush.

___ Is worth more than $200.

___ Was decorated with a slip cup.

___ Would be classified as a jar.

16. This collection of baskets is worth at least $3000.

　　True ___　False ___

A.

B.

C.

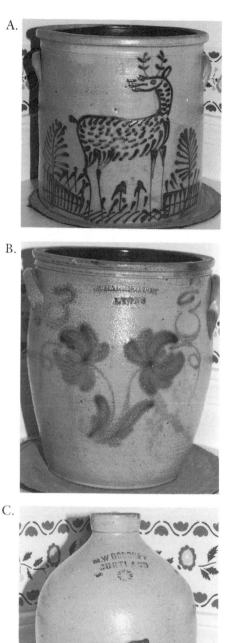

17. There is no cheese basket in this collection.

   True ___ False ___

18. The basket with the handle, in the lower left of the picture, was used in gathering apples.

   True ___ False ___

19. A piece of stoneware that is described as "pear-shaped" could also be called ___ .

20. Almost all commercially made Shaker rocking chairs were made in ___ , New York.

21. Troy and Ft. Edward were famous locations for stoneware potteries in the state of ___ .

22. An individual who travels throughout a given geographic area buying antiques and reselling them to dealers is known as a ___ .

Estimate the Values

Match the value with the description of the piece of furniture that is described below.

23. ___ Refinished pine pie safe, machine stamped tins, one drawer, c. 1900.

24. ___ Walnut step-back cupboard, "blind front," raised panel doors, c. 1850.

25. ___ Blue painted dry sink, pine, original condition with zinc liner, Pennsylvania, c. 1840.

26. ___ Heavily overpainted deacon's bench or settle, original condition, c. late nineteenth century, 14' long.
   a. $2200   b. $525
   c. $750   d. $1500

Essay

1. As has been discussed in class at length, the dry sink is the end product of the natural evolution of the bucket bench. List two other pieces of country furniture eagerly collected today that have also evolved.

2. Erik Estrada and Troy Donahue were in an antiques shop in Fargo, North Dakota, while on a motorcycle trip across America. They purchased an oak church pew, some carnival glass, and a pair of vintage boxer shorts. If the total bill was $236.89, how much were the shorts?

Answers

Qualifying Examination

1. smalls

2. picker

3. glazed

4. pieced out

5. late or low end

6. late or low end

7. early bird

Final Examination

1. a

2. c

3. c

4. c

5. a or b

6. a

7. b

8. b, d, f

9. false—Gould didn't write books on furniture.

10. false

11. false—Massachusetts

12. false

13. false

14. In blue paint it's worth at least $225
The handle was hand carved.
The basket could be from as late as 1900.

15. a, c, b, c, a and c, b

16. true

17. true

18. true

19. ovoid

20. Mt. Lebanon

21. New York

22. picker

23. b

24. d

25. a

26. c

Interpreting Your Test Results

36–40 points: The president of the High Achiever's Club will personally install a direct telephone line to your home. This will allow him to stay in constant contact with you. Please *do not* eat for two hours prior to a prescheduled presidential call.

26–35 points: The former Pinky's Place of Peculiar Pleasures, Crafts, and Collectibles in Picayune, Mississippi will be deeded to you (when Pinky is paroled on 2-14-97 there is some potential for conflict)

16–25 points: Your name will be added to the Honored Guests Plaque on the wall of the Sunset Smorgasbord in downtown Mogadishu, Somalia

10–15 points: You are assigned remedial reading of all previous editions of this book.